EBURY PRESS

I AM NO MESSIAH

Sonu Sood is an international film actor, producer, entrepreneur and social worker. He has won several awards for his work in films. He is also the recipient of the United Nations Development Programme's SDG Action Award for his humanitarian work during the COVID-19 pandemic. The stories of his migrant rescue mission feature in school texts in Andhra Pradesh as lessons in ethics. A fitness enthusiast with exemplary people skills, Sonu is now a household name. He resides in Mumbai with his wife, Sonali, and their two sons, Eshaan and Ayaan.

Meena K. Iyer was the editor of *Bombay Times*, a film critic at the *Times of India* and edited *DNA After Hrs*. She has been an active media professional for the last thirty-nine years and co-authored Rishi Kapoor's bestselling book, *Khullam Khulla: Rishi Kapoor Uncensored*. She resides in Mumbai and is currently heading a film company.

With Compliments

KHIMJI®

Since 1936

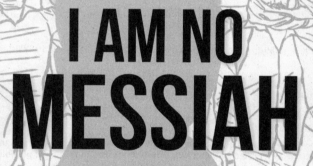

I AM NO MESSIAH

Happy Reading love.

Sonu Sood

SONU SOOD
with MEENA K. IYER

EBURY
PRESS

An imprint of Penguin Random House

EBURY PRESS

USA | Canada | UK | Ireland | Australia
New Zealand | India | South Africa | China

Ebury Press is part of the Penguin Random House group of companies
whose addresses can be found at global.penguinrandomhouse.com

Published by Penguin Random House India Pvt. Ltd
7th Floor, Infinity Tower C, DLF Cyber City,
Gurgaon 122 002, Haryana, India

Penguin
Random House
India

First published in Ebury Press by Penguin Random House India 2020

ISBN 9780143451983

Typeset in Adobe Garamond Pro by Manipal Technologies Limited, Manipal
Printed at Thomson Press India Ltd, New Delhi

www.penguin.co.in

MIX
Paper
FSC FSC® C010615

To my parents, Saroj and Shakti

'It's impossible,' said Pride
'It's risky,' said Experience
'It's pointless,' said Reason
'Give it a try,' whispered the Heart

Contents

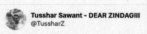

Tusshar Sawant - DEAR ZINDAGIII
@TussharZ

@SonuSood Dear sir u don't know how amazing ur going out of your way to care about others, sharing strength, love in way lifting spirits and touch hearts thank u, sir, for helping me in taking care of my daughter Shaurya Sawant medical expense. A lot of blessings to u sir.

12:48 PM · Sep 4, 2020 · Twitter for Android

183 Retweets   **3** Quote Tweets   **2.6K** Likes

Akshay AgraWal
@akkiagrawal5

Sonu Sood launches 'ILAAJ India' initiative
uniindia.com/~/sonu-sood-la… @SonuSood @ketto
#ilaajindiainitiative #SonuSood #ketto

One more Great thing by a Great Person 🙏 love you sir

Saroj gupta
@Sarojgu59106057

Thanks a lot for helping me. I am very lucky that I got a chance to work with Sonu Sena. I am very much thankful to Sonu Sir and Nand Ahuja Sir..#sonusena
@Nand20Ahuja @SonuSood

Vidya Pratap
@VidyaPratap6

Thanku so much @SonuSood sir 🙏🙏for everything you are our real life hero thnqq so much 🖤🖤 #travelingstart #forindiabihar ✈️✈️#kyrgyzstan 📷to #india 🚂#mission successful 🏆🏆@flyspicejet @ashma_pm @NeetiGoel2 @vishallamba20

10:38 PM · Jul 26, 2020 from Kyrgyzstan · Twitter for iPhone

195 Retweets   **6** Quote Tweets   **1.4K** Likes

Introduction

'Messiah of the Migrants'

It brings a faint blush to my face when such titles are bestowed on me. But when I pause on the highway of life, quite literally as you will agree, I realize that nobody transmutes overnight to become deserving of such an honour.

I, for sure, know that I didn't.

On Wednesday, 15 April 2020, it was that nudge from my heart which sent me to that traffic junction in 400605, the zip code of Kalwa in Thane district, with a mask on my face. That spot was the Bodhi tree of my life. It was where I received my enlightenment.

I shudder to imagine how empty my life would have been if I, too, had chosen to continue basking in that overwhelming attention and affection that we film stars receive. But it was as if destiny had willed that I had to go beyond stardom to find my raison d'etre. In fact, I had to use my stardom to discover why karma had placed me in a position of power so that I could use it altruistically.

I found my karma on the streets of Mumbai during the lockdown imposed after the outbreak of the COVID-19 pandemic, when I personally went to distribute truckloads of food packets and other basic essentials to migrant workers.

Nothing indeed comes from a place of contentment. Every human being is always going through some upheaval within. But while inner turmoil can be bothersome, it can also help a person go down an untried, fulfilling path—the road less travelled.

For me, the outcome of that emotional turbulence was an awakening of the conscience. When the pandemic struck, the first few days of March flew by for me, like for everyone else, in a state of slumber. I was lulled into a kind of obedience to just follow the rules. COVID-19 was a mystery disease; it was a hidden enemy. No one knew where the monster lurked, how or whom it would strike. Perhaps we'll never fully comprehend the truth behind the virus that brought the world to its knees.

But after the first couple of weeks of sanitizers, handwashes, face masks, hand gloves and staying home safe, I began to feel a distinct sense of unease. I have always been a man of action and commitment; I was not cut out for indolence and apathy. I am a man on the move, not an inert, lethargic being. My conscience sent heartfelt messages to my mind, which in turn churned with thoughts. What I was sure of and knew straight off was that I wasn't meant to sit complacently at home.

I subjected myself to my own version of a SWOT self-assessment—strengths, weaknesses, opportunities and threats.

The weakness: I was not a man of medicine, a qualified doctor, a health-care worker or even a compounder. The opportunity was right before me. The world outside my door was caught in a grip of bewilderment. I had to do something about it, and I had to go out there and be a front-line worker. The threats or obstacles: I had no clue what they would be. But they could never be a deterrent in my life. Not after the trial by fire that a struggler goes through before finding stardom.

One of my strengths was that I was unafraid of facing the unknown, confident about overcoming hurdles and taking them head-on. The clincher was a dialogue I had with myself; I had a conversation with my conscience. I asked what my biggest unique strength was and received the answer: I was a celebrity. People knew me, they recognized my face, and my name could open doors. I had the distinct advantage of being able to stand beside a stranger in need and give him the reassuring comfort that I was watching out for him.

My Kalinga Moment

What prompted me to drive down to Kalwa Chowk in Thane and oversee the distribution in person when I could have easily dispatched our truckloads of food, drinking water, sanitizers and sanitary napkins without leaving home? What drove me out when I could have sat home feeling virtuous? The answer to that was an inexplicable restlessness inside me. I couldn't be content using my reach as a celebrity only to post 'stay safe' and 'wash your hands' messages on social media. I couldn't just upload morale-boosting videos on how to stay mentally and physically fit during the lockdown. I had to be personally out there, on the battlefront. It was like a call from the divine that drew me where I was meant to go.

I had responded to that conscience call earlier too, in a smaller measure, when I handed over Shakti Sagar, my six-storey hotel in Juhu, to the state authorities in April, two weeks after a nationwide lockdown had been announced. Health-care workers were the wall between us and the virus. Giving them food and a place to rest in the rooms of Shakti Sagar, a building with a name of special significance to me, pleased me, and I was glad when other colleagues from cinema followed suit by similarly throwing open their properties to the corona warriors. Buying this building on 24 May 2018 had been, for me, a confirmation that I'd reached a place of worth in life—an achievement that I had earned and not inherited from a big-name production house. It's a story I shall soon share, but naming the building after my late father, Shakti Sagar, was particularly gratifying. It was as if my parents were looking down from heaven and guiding me to do what they'd always taught me to do—help people.

The very first time that I stepped out to distribute food packets to migrant workers during the lockdown, my wife, Sonali, asked me, 'Sonu, where are you off to?' She reminded me that a lockdown meant staying at home. That was on 15 April. I placated her by saying that it was personally very important for me to do this, and she relented.

And thank God I took that step. That day, 15 April, was my Kalinga moment, when life, as with Emperor Ashoka, put me on a course I had never thought was on my itinerary.

In the past, I had heard people talk about 'finding their calling' and saying, 'Hey, this is what I was destined to do.'

I knew of friends who said they had found their calling in politics or teaching or something else. I know of people who had switched careers midstream. When any of them told me, 'Sonu, I have found my path', I would be happy for them but couldn't help feeling a little suspicious. Does something really come calling you? Is it an inward or outward sign? Do you get hit in the middle of your life with a purpose?

But now that it has happened to me, I know that all of us have been placed in this world to do what destiny has planned for us. You never know when that plan will be rolled out, when that plan will call out to you.

I've been in the Indian film industry for close to two decades. I've worked in countless films in different languages around the globe. Responsibility and commitment have been the bywords of my life. And I know the worth of a promise, the value of my word.

I have worked in films, I have produced films, I have dabbled in real estate, I have done myriad things in my life. But the soul-uplifting joy and satisfaction I got from my 'Ghar Bhejo' initiative, which consumed my life for almost three months, defies description. It felt as if my whole life had been leading to this. As if I had travelled from Moga to Mumbai, going through hoops of fire to become an actor, a superstar and a man of steel, only to one day transform into a figure of hope who came in from nowhere to lift truckloads of strangers and carry them home.

When I could take a moment to reflect on this course-altering phase, I realized that the solicitude, the sense of purpose and compassion of such magnitude had to have been stirred in me at a young age. This was where my parents played the most important part in my upbringing. There is a saying that children close their ears to advice but open their eyes to example.

When I stood on that highway to flag off busloads of worried and harried workers, who just wanted to go home, the scene resonated with what I had witnessed, catalogued and filed away in my childhood memories.

I was weaned on the gregarious and generous spirit of the Punjabi household. Our doors were always open and the dining table always had more than just our nuclear family around it. Hospitality, sharing your roti with others, is an organic Punjabi trait. There is a tradition in most of our homes to welcome people to our table, with *ghar ka khana* and *khaoji* being our favourite phrases. Our kitchens are our pride. The more people we feed, the better we sleep. Usually with a beatific smile on the face and warmth nestled deep inside the heart.

My mother and father instilled a basic life lesson in me. They told me that no matter where I was, or at what stage in life, I should consider myself worthy only if I were able to help someone less privileged than me. But I must confess that at no stage had I ever envisioned that I would one day play a role in a campaign with such social ramifications as the Ghar Bhejo movement. I had never dreamt that I would be a part of something so substantial. But then, even science fiction of the *Contagion* variety couldn't have imagined a worldwide lockdown of this proportion, or what it would do to a workforce that found itself stranded on the roads.

If I had given in to the celebrity syndrome of sitting in my ivory tower and having my largesse delivered to the needy by remote control, I would never have come face to face with the trauma of the migrant workers or understood that a food packet was a woefully inadequate substitute for a ride back home.

When my neighbour Ajay Dhama drove me down to Thane that day, I comforted myself with the thought that I'd be doing the soul-cleansing service of distributing food packets and other essentials among the migrants, who were meant to walk all the way back to their villages. But I was unprepared for what lay before me. It was despair—up, close, personal and disturbing.

There was confusion and chaos, emotional and practical. Thousands had begun their *padyatras*, their long journeys on foot, some cradling children in their arms, others carrying their elders on their shoulders. Husbands walked ahead, holding tiffin carriers and water bottles. Wives followed, their heads covered with the sari or dupatta, holding their children, bracing themselves for the harshness of the sun and the darkness of the night.

We encountered a medley of deeply perturbed faces drawn, none of them wearing a smile, not even one of hope. People from various castes, regions and professions were present. Some willingly put out their hands for the food we were distributing. Others hesitated. Their gaze held several unasked questions. Perhaps it was my imagination at work, but I was hit by this disconcerting feeling that someone in that crowd was asking me, 'Do you really think that by handing out these packets, you've done enough? You've assuaged your soul?' It was my mind playing tricks, my conscience rubbing its eyes and waking up. No one asked me any questions. It tickled them to find a face they recognized, a celebrity in their midst. But honestly, beyond that my presence gave them nothing.

Something that struck me, and is stuck in my mind even now, was the vast sea of humanity before me. I was, at first, taken aback by the sheer number of people on the roads. Innumerable people on the highway, below bridges, on the sidewalks, social distancing a distant dream. Some were squatting, others standing, restless and yet resigned to their fate.

For distribution at Kalwa Chowk, we had carried a couple of truckloads of food, water and basic essentials for 48,000–50,000 people. On average, we were handing out two packets to each person when some of the migrant workers requested me for enough food to tide them over for ten days. It seemed odd to me that they were asking me for food that would last so long. So I asked them, 'Why would you want food for ten days?' They explained that they were going on foot to their homes in Karnataka, a journey of at least ten days. And it was then that the reality of their ordeal hit me. It stumped me. There were 350 people there, all set to walk home.

'I met a family with an elderly lady and a little girl. When I asked them where they were going, they said, Karnataka. I told them to hold on for two days; I would see what I could do. And thus began the chain to set the whole process in motion,' I said to senior journalist and author Bharathi S. Pradhan, for her Sunday column in the *Telegraph*.

The number 350 was just the beginning. There were thousands more waiting in hope, because as the days passed, more and more people came to Kalwa Chowk, which was a kind of stopover on their journey by foot. There were batches heading in different directions to Bihar, Uttar Pradesh, Jharkhand and other states.

'Ask not what your country can do for you; ask what you can do for your country.' Inspired by John F. Kennedy's epochal words, a transformative thought began to take shape inside my head. For one thing, it became amply clear to me, and I admitted it to myself, that what I was doing was definitely neither adequate nor a solution to the real problem that loomed large on the highway. I couldn't possibly sit back smugly about distributing 'brown paper packages tied up with strings'.

The corollary to the first thought was that newfound wisdom had to translate into action. My strength, my star power, the privileged position of being a public face had to be put to worthwhile use.

Once I'd cleared my head, I dialled Neeti Goel, a restaurateur-friend who became a front-foot player alongside me in the movement. Putting two heads together instead of relying on one was the wiser way of coming up with a practical, doable plan to provide the right salve for stranded migrant workers. In the course of my conversations with her and a couple of other friends, I decided I was going to stick my neck out and go the whole hog.

I was going to put wheels under the feet of the people who wanted to go home. When I asked the workers who were going to Karnataka to give me two days to find them a better way of reaching their destinations than journeying on foot, they were at first mistrustful. They had been left to their own devices and were so helpless that they didn't dare to even hope someone cared enough to actually shepherd them home.

They were impatient, they were disbelieving. Many said they would walk home. Others told me they would cycle all the way. Realizing how onerous the task before me was, I requested them to be patient with me. I put my persuasive powers to good use, assuring them that though it would take a couple of days for me to organize a ride for them, it would come through. I would make sure I got them to their destinations more comfortably than they could imagine.

It was an impromptu but impassioned plea. And, like Shah Rukh Khan's dressing-room speech in *Chak De! India*, it had an impact. They agreed to wait and gave me a chance to prove that I meant what I said.

With many of them, I had a one-on-one conversation. I conveyed to them that they were the heartbeat of our nation. I said, 'You helped build our bridges, roads, homes, hospitals, religious places, schools and even our courts. It is your sweat and blood that has gone into our infrastructure. Today, when you are literally standing stranded on the crossroads, fearing there is no one here for you, I'm with you. The least I can do is to flag off your journey.'

The visuals of crowds stretching for miles—of lockdown-beaten migrants walking homewards, families moving en masse with the elderly who could barely walk—made it difficult for me to shut my eyes. Sleep played hide-and-seek with me as I became more aware of what was happening out there on the roads of my country, my state, my city.

Questions that whirred in my head: How could we allow those who helped build our homes to not reach their own homes? How could we turn away unaffected from their trauma, as if it had little to do with us?

American entertainer Lily Tomlin was spot on when she said: 'I always wondered why somebody doesn't do something about that. Then I realized I was somebody.' I realized that I was not merely somebody but a fortunate somebody who had a voice and the means to 'do something about that'.

But, as I told Lachmi Deb Roy of *Outlook* magazine, 'Initially, I didn't have any idea how to make arrangements to send migrant labourers home.' I had sheltered the first 350 in a school, having promised them that I would personally organize buses to ferry them home. I also assured them that they would get food and other amenities while they waited for the transport to arrive.

This was where the Ghar Bhejo movement, the 'Send Them Home' mission, really began. At that juncture, I didn't know how far or how wide the movement would carry. But carry it did.

As the movement gained momentum, and word spread like wildfire that I was not making empty promises but was actually making transport available for migrants, they came in droves, looking for me and my representatives. Hundreds of requests came each day, thousands each week. My inbox and WhatsApp messages overflowed. At one stage, my inbox had over 3500 mails from various people. I don't know where they got my email ID from, but I was inundated with mails and started to lose track. Neeti, Sonali, my kids, everybody joined in. My chartered accountant, Pankaj Jalisatgi, stepped in with his team of four. The four multiplied into twelve Ghar Bhejo volunteers.

The first obstacle was obtaining permission from the different states. For the first busload, we had to get permissions from the relevant authorities in Maharashtra, where the migrants would begin their journey on sturdy wheels, and from Karnataka, which would receive them. The catch was that most states did not want to accept people from Maharashtra, because this was a red zone, with the highest number of cases and high infection rates. We surmounted that difficulty by getting every passenger on the bus tested for the virus and getting doctors' certificates for them all. This may sound easy on paper, but it was a project in itself.

Even within Mumbai, while the buses waited, fully tanked and ready to roll, workers from containment areas, like Worli, couldn't step out and reach the bus stop; they were pushed back to where they'd been stranded since the lockdown began on 24 March 2020. We desperately needed state cooperation to send our migrants safely home.

There's much wisdom wrapped around many a saying about taking that small first step which could end up as the biggest leap of your life. But Martin Luther King Jr's 'Faith is taking that first step even when you can't see the whole staircase' comes closest to describing how a leap of faith works best when you're in that confounding state of figuring out what the first step should be.

I went about it with an engineer's precision. As they say, education is never a waste, and my four years at the Yeshwantrao Chavan College of Engineering (YCCE) in Nagpur came in handy. I made a road map. Since I had no experience in executing something on this scale, I brought in more of my friends. We needed more heads, more hands.

Apart from certificates from doctors for those leaving the state, we needed to establish a line of communication with assistant magistrates, district magistrates, deputy commissioners of police and a roster of other officials. It was imperative to make contact with a wide range of authorities to ensure smooth transition from one state to another.

We needed to familiarize ourselves with guidelines; each state had its own. A glitch-free journey for migrant workers had to be firmed up, because they were in no position to explain anything to anybody confronting them. Most of them were so shaken up that they just wanted a smooth passage home, with no questions asked. This put additional responsibility on my team and me, because I needed to be one hundred per cent sure that our arrangements were legitimate and efficient.

Our responsibility went beyond bidding each migrant worker goodbye in Mumbai. After they left Maharashtra, we had to see to it that they reached their doorstep safe and sound. I actually spoke to cops patrolling borders and on expressway check *nakas* (points) to make sure that the transport carrying the migrants went through without a snag. Initially, there were a few hiccups, but we learnt about and rectified them as we went along, until we got the hang of it. It also took a while for security personnel in all states to understand the integrity and intention behind the whole movement. It was heartening as their understanding grew into admiration and cooperation, indeed into enthusiastic participation.

We started at point zero and got ourselves a toll-free number. Next, apart from arranging for ten buses to make interstate road trips from Maharashtra to Karnataka, we had to connect with government officials at both ends of the journey.

Karmic Connections

If you take a breather and care to notice, at many points in your life, you'll understand why life dealt you certain cards which seemed baffling to you at one time. It was only after the beginning of the Ghar Bhejo movement that I realized why karma had given me stardom in the three southern states of Tamil Nadu, Karnataka and Andhra Pradesh. Today, because of the volume of work I had done in Karnataka, I have a lot of friends there, men of influence who could open bureaucratic doors and get us the required permissions from government offices.

Once the permissions came through, our energy levels shot up, and we became determined to bring this daunting task to fruition.

The journey began with the first step of 350 migrant labourers who reached home safely. But there were thousands more yearning to go back to their small towns and villages. Connections had to be established with many more state governments—UP, Bihar, Jharkhand, Odisha, Rajasthan. Multitudes had their homes in other states—Tamil Nadu, Andhra Pradesh, Telangana. But we could ply buses only to those states that allowed them entry.

The 350 burgeoned into over 1 lakh who had to be transported to their homes. The government gave us Shramik Specials to move many more by train. But the clamour for buses continued. We had to open up airports and, within a given window of time, book flights to carry the distressed from one end of the country to the other. And there were lakhs still seeking help. Ghar Bhejo was an uninterrupted exercise until the last person who wanted to go home was reunited with their family. In the process, I came off as some superhero, as a messiah of the migrants. But it's teamwork that lifts the trophy. I just chipped in.

The paperwork piled up. Ghar Bhejo required tons of paperwork—a friend in the restaurant business took over and helped me deal with it. It was like a war room. As the juggernaut moved to many more states and more modes of transport, my wife, Sonali, segregated people state-wise and lists were drawn up. Buses had their own limitations—because of social distancing, you couldn't pack them to capacity. So alternatives also had to be explored.

I couldn't possibly keep track of every person who was reaching out to me and coordinate their travel plans. Neeti Goel walked every step of the way with me. Pankaj Jalisatgi fine-tuned which batch would travel by bus, who'd get on to the Shramik Specials arranged by the Centre and who needed to be airlifted. Friend and film-maker Farah Khan called frequently to inquire how she could pitch in and organized water for the travellers. Other friends volunteered to pick up migrants from different parts of Mumbai and bring them to the bus stop.

Once the crucial first move was made, the whole chain began to fall into place.

As someone said, 'The two most important days of your life are the day you are born and the day you find out why.'

I was born on 30 July 1973, a Monday, the first important day of my life. On 15 April 2020, a Wednesday, I found out why. It was the second most important day of my life. A day to be marked on my personal calendar for posterity.

The first time the rest of the world learnt of Ghar Bhejo was when I flagged off the first ten busloads with 350 anxious passengers going home to Karnataka. Every day that I stepped out to facilitate this journey, my family worried about me. At the outset, Sonali attempted to dissuade me from going out to a public space, and tried to convince me to do what I wanted behind closed doors. It was natural for her to worry about my safety and well-being, with a pandemic raging outside. But I had a hunch that my presence would make a difference to the embattled people who were on the cusp of a long journey. I knew that the solace my flesh-and-blood presence would give them, as I walked shoulder to shoulder with them, was irreplaceable.

Instinct told me once again that my personal, physical presence would make a difference to the people who had lived through a harrowing period and needed to see some light at the end of the tunnel. So seeing a reassuring figure standing by those buses, seeing someone they recognized and trusted bidding them goodbye was something they could hold on to and draw comfort from. It was an image they would carry with them back home—a sort of insurance that gave them the confidence to believe better days awaited them. To see me pad up and go to the public crease gave my wife the expected jitters. But I was the captain of my team: my presence in person was imperative and irreplaceable.

It went a long way in building the confidence of the stranded, who knew that here was a man they could reach out to. And their numbers swelled. When people realized they could get to me even through Twitter, I started getting messages in the thousands on my timeline. Since the migrants themselves were not on social media, they would get strangers to pass on the messages to me. There were appeals from random people informing me that a group of ten migrants was stuck in some odd place and requesting me to arrange transport for them.

Logic, Logistics and Statistics

At one point, there were 1.5 lakh requests, either through mail or social media or our toll-free number. It was hard for all of us to cope with the growing numbers, but ultimately, we devised a way to categorize the requests as 'Crucial', 'Urgent' and 'Moderately Urgent'. Once the listings were made, we swung into action.

Emergencies came under 'Crucial'. People stuck on highways, without shelter and money, were labelled 'Urgent'. Through this classification system, we were able to bring order to our operation.

It was a humungous, non-stop process as we got calls to rescue people from dhabas outside Haryana, on the highways of Uttar Pradesh and Rajasthan. Sometimes, people just stood at petrol pumps and sent us the zip codes, asking for vehicles.

As the movement grew and went beyond Mumbai, friends from Lucknow, Kanpur and other cities came forward to help. They drove to the main nakas or city centres to meet groups of people who had been travelling on foot and took them to shelters, like schools, wedding halls or some such place that was opened up to take them in. They were given food and taken care of while we organized their transport after getting all the required details of each group.

The logistics were like we were going into a battle, and we needed an army of supporters. We got buses and, in some cases, truck drivers to help transport people, and petrol pumps on highways became pick-up points.

There was a time when people even found out my residential address in Mumbai and had begun hanging out in the lanes outside. Groups of forty-five to fifty people would gather outside Casablanca, the building where I reside in Mumbai, asking for transport. I was worried for their safety and was also beset with doubt over my ability to send home so many at one go. But my team and I never gave up. We found a way to break up the groups into smaller ones, and we kept finding modes of transport to get them out of Mumbai.

If Ghar Bhejo by bus was a logistical challenge, the railways came with their own set of impediments. Buses had their limitations because of social distancing, which meant that they couldn't ply to their full capacity. So we had to turn to trains. One trainload could carry over 1200 passengers. But experience taught us that road transport was relatively easier to organize, because a private citizen can't just book an entire train, especially during a pandemic. Being a government-run mode of transport, trains meant mounds of paperwork to tackle, with permissions required from the state administration, central government and railway authorities. Coordinating between all of them felt like scaling Mount Everest. But again, it got easier as we came to grips with what it entailed.

Each train could ideally pack in 1200 people, but sometimes, I would send as many as 1600 on a train, because there was a human tidal wave waiting to be sent home.

How's the Josh?

At one point I thought aloud, 'I wish I had a *jaadu ki chhadi*, a magic wand, to send them all home.'

Our responsibility stretched beyond seeing off a train from Mumbai Central or VT. Shramik Specials made very few stops. Keeping the food supply going to every passenger we sent home was another challenge. There had to be detailed coordination with volunteers and contacts, at junctions like Ratlam and Vadodara, who would meet the trains and give food and water to the migrants.

To add to the COVID-19 pandemic and lockdown woes, a cyclone was headed towards the coast of Mumbai on 1 June 2020. Moving people as Cyclone Nisarga threatened to hit Maharashtra was even more exacting, as they had to be provided with food, shelter and comforting words. They were worried because the few trains that had been green-signalled were cancelled and so were other means of transport.

The cry for help came from different places. A group of people, originally from Assam, sent me a photograph of them standing at Lokmanya Tilak Bridge near the Kurla terminus in Mumbai. With the weatherman forecasting the fury of Nisarga, these people had no place, no transport, no food. It was an SOS we had to respond to. Food was an immediate requirement, which was met without delay. We fed those people under the bridge and asked them to bear with us till we found suitable shelter for them. The circumstances were beyond us as the weather added to our difficulties. We couldn't arrange any kind of transport in those conditions and had to keep the group safe for four days before I could put them all on a flight to Guwahati and heave a sigh of relief. Similarly, another lot of migrants was flown to Uttarakhand.

But each time I waved a batch of people goodbye, I got a reward. The smile that had eluded them for weeks lit up their faces and tears of hope replaced despair in their eyes.

My josh, my energy was almost unflagging. People had to be picked up in tempo travellers, from Palghar, Nalasopara and far-flung areas, in the dead of night and transported to a bus terminus or railway station. All this while taking precautionary measures, like getting every vehicle sanitized after each group had exited it. I did a lot of this myself because volunteers were not always available at those unearthly hours.

'Service to others is the rent you pay for your room here on earth,' said Muhammad Ali. The champ of the boxing ring certainly knew what he was talking about, because paying my 'rent' showed me what reservoirs of energy I had stored within me. I was never exhausted; I was supercharged, like a man possessed. I became busier than I ever had been before the lockdown. Many a time, I put in twenty hours of uninterrupted work, barely sleeping. In fact, ever since Ghar Bhejo began, I've been checking my messages till 2.30–3 a.m. daily, catching literally just forty winks and waking up by 5.30 a.m., because the first batch of migrants would usually be sent off between 6–6.30 a.m. It has been a round-the-clock obsession but never a cause for complaint for the exhilarating contentment it has given me.

Waving off a batch of my migrant 'family' was only the beginning of an association with each one, as there were unending follow-ups from them. It was their sheer gratitude and love that made them send me the pictures from their journey, looking forward to at least an emoji from me in acknowledgement. When they reached their homes, the flurry of phone calls continued. I would receive pictures and videos of them at home. They didn't want to cut their links with me even after they were home. They wanted me to see their families. It was as if they had adopted me to be a part of their lives.

It was impossible to snap ties with them after a happy send-off, and their messages gave me joy. I also felt that I should stay in touch until the newly forged ties reached their natural conclusion. I knew that once they settled down to a routine, got wrapped up in their jobs, they would be slowly and organically weaned away from their dependence on me. I thus stayed connected to thousands of them, because to many of them and to me, this connection could not be severed the moment they reached their doorstep.

A Platter of Roles

The fact that those who had been strangers until yesterday included me in their lives made me feel that I had done something right. But these after-journey connections were maintained alongside our work of coordinating, planning and taking care of the next batch of people who were looking for my help. I was on my toes all through the lockdown months. Some of the migrant workers who reached home weeks ago continue to send me text messages. It has taken enormous amounts of my time and attention to maintain communication with them, but I have tried to keep their spirits up by replying to each of them, at least for the initial period until they settled down.

Many of my colleagues from the entertainment industry have also opened their hearts and their wallets in different ways during this unprecedented crisis. Mine hasn't been the only spectacular effort, but it has given me a purpose in life. Amid the mayhem of an intense pandemic, I was able to hew myself a clear path that actually mapped a way for 1 lakh of the stranded migrants to go home.

At times, taking care of them even meant, for me, switching roles from a trip adviser or travel agent to a shrink and counsellor. I got some really way-out travel requests, and I tried to humour these, if only to help people keep their chins up during such a difficult period. An unusual one came from a man who said, 'Sonu bhai, I'm stuck, I need to go to a wine shop.' To him, I jocularly replied, 'Sorry bhai, I can't get you to a wine shop now. However, after you reach home, you can find your own way to a bar. And God forbid, if you end up having one too many, perhaps I can find a way to send you home from the bar.'

There was one couple that seemed to have unresolved differences. Both husband and wife reached out to me and said, 'Bhai, send us home.' And then the wife added, 'But I want to go to my mother's house. I can't stay with him.' To them, I wisecracked, 'Perhaps I can send both of you to Goa to sort out your differences.'

I had to thus play innumerable roles in dealing with the migrants whose requests ranged from simple ones, like 'Please send us home', to complex ones, like 'I need to get away from my in-laws'. I had to be on the ball to volley the right reply to each of them.

Months have gone by, and I have sent thousands home, but there are times when I still wake up with a start because the early images of that tsunami of the young and the ageing, all weather-beaten and walking on the highway, are impossible to delete from my memory. You keep asking yourself, 'Is there really so much suffering in the world?' You look around, sense the comfort of family and feel gratitude spring within you. We are privileged and we need to say grace many times a day. We have no idea what a harsh world exists out there and how protected we have been. Every time you sit at the dining table, think of the countless millions for whom two square meals and a roof over their heads is an unimaginable luxury and be grateful for what you have.

I thought I'd come to Mumbai to chase an impossible dream. But I now believe that I was propelled to this city to fulfil a purpose. I am thankful for becoming the catalyst in the lives of so many migrants. My heart beats in Mumbai, but after Ghar Bhejo, I have begun to feel that a part of me lives in the villages of UP, Bihar, Jharkhand, Assam, Uttarakhand and various other states where I now have new friends.

Poster Boy

When I took my baby steps in the film industry, I must confess that it bothered my parents to see me get barely any mention on a poster or hoarding. As parents are wont to be, they wanted to see me get equal prominence alongside the big marquee names. They were somewhat mollified when I later graduated to getting equal billing in promotional material. But my father would sometimes say wistfully, 'One day, I know you'll get top billing.' It didn't happen in his lifetime, but I can modestly accept that the kind of write-ups and prominence I have got for pioneering Ghar Bhejo would have made my parents burst with pride. That's why I so often say that I think it's two people up in heaven who have made my mission happen here on earth.

On 17 May 2020, the intrepid journalist Barkha Dutt tweeted: 'The Power of One. @actorSonuSood (also aided by his friend Neeti) sends hundreds of migrant workers home, first to Karnataka and now to UP. One bus costs anywhere between 65,000 to 2 lakh rupees . . . Sonu Sood uses personal funds to send migrant workers home.'

At that point, Barkha herself had been on the road for over fifty days and more—in fact, all through the lockdown—recording the plight of those who sought to go home on foot. About alleviating their pain, she said to me, 'You feel helpless because you cannot give a lift to one worker out of a whole group.' The sheer logistics was intimidating to all. That was where I was blessed to step in. It was both a huge challenge and a massive responsibility. But it was an unseen power that was making it all happen, with me as the medium. We are but His mere tools.

There were articles written about the 'Reel-Life Villain' proving to be a 'Real-Life Hero'. And then came the memes and cartoons. From calling me the 'Asli Bahubali' and 'vaccine for migrants' to sketches of me as a caped superhero. There were cartoons that had world-renowned superheroes of all shapes, heights and colours lined up on both sides, bowing to Sonu Sood. A superman pushing a train full of migrants to Varanasi; a masked superhero flying with migrants on his back; even a naughty one, of a wife caught in action with another man asking her husband, 'But you said you were stuck in Mumbai.' And the husband replying, 'Sonu Sood sent me home.'

'*Paidal kyun jaoge mere dost?*' became the new tag line as a cartoonist drew a superhero looming above tiny migrants on the road with the words, '*Paidal kyun jaoge mere dost*? Why would you walk home, my friend?' The avalanche of encouragement was overwhelming, far more humbling than an Oscar win. But I had miles to go before I could sleep. Or take a bow.

After 45,000 on a single day, I lost count of the thousands of parcels of food and essentials that our team had been distributing right from Ramzan. The pandemic months were also tough on my family. While I got my share of hugs and kisses on a regular basis from Sonali and my sons, Eshaan (eighteen) and Ayaan (eleven), they also felt that I was disconnected from them because of my preoccupation with the migrants' cause. They understood that it was for the greater good, but on some occasions they would say, 'Dad, you have no time for us.' Sonali constantly worried about my well-being, and my odd sleeping pattern disturbed her.

I realized one morning that they were not wrong in complaining. I was so involved in my mission that there were long stretches of time, sometimes two to three days, when I didn't even speak to any of them. But, as always, my family continued to be my support system. They were more anxious about my welfare than demanding, and it became a family affair when Eshaan and Ayaan were given the task of reading the huge pile of letters we received and making short reports on them. They also helped with the timetables for buses, adding remarks on which bus would stop at which dhaba. My family thus joined the task force and also became champions of the cause.

Yet there were many hurdles. Due to the lockdown, it was difficult to get eateries to open and supply breakfast, lunch and dinner to the travellers. I had to sometimes use my 'star power' to request dhaba owners to open their kitchens at 6 a.m. just to serve a busload of passengers.

But, as it happens with any mass movement, along with the applause and the accolades, there had to be some derision too. It started with the utterly incredible rumour that I had orchestrated Ghar Bhejo to fuel my entry into politics. I don't know why it's so difficult for people to accept an altruistic act for what it truly is and not hunt around for imagined motives.

Mission Apolitical

Let me be unequivocal about it. I am not predisposed towards politics of any hue. A lot of people have suggested that I should get into the political fray; they say this presumably because they want to have someone out there who's genuinely wired to do good work for the country. However, at the moment, I'm not inclined to go down that path. I have no clue what the future has in store for me, but I do know that Ghar Bhejo was not my entry ticket into politics. The cause of the migrants has been a conscience call. I helped and I will continue to help them. I'm committed to it for life.

Besides this mission, my heart ticks only for the movies. I love cinema, I enjoy acting. I would rather concentrate on my acting career than get drawn into politics at this stage of my life.

Perhaps the rumour was set off because during Ghar Bhejo I had interacted in different ways with a slew of politicians. On 7 June 2020, I had a non-political meeting with the chief minister of Maharashtra, Uddhav Thackeray. That very morning, his newspaper, *Saamana*, had published a scathing editorial by member of Parliament Sanjay Raut. I didn't read it, but I had a lot of people calling me that day, seeking my reaction to the piece. I didn't wish to comment on it or get drawn into a futile controversy when I had my hands full organizing travel for nearly 6000-odd migrants. However, later in the day, MLA Aslam Shaikh from the Indian National Congress, who's a friend of mine, told me that we should definitely meet Uddhavji and his son, Aaditya Thackeray. So that night, I went to Matoshree, the Thackeray residence, to meet our CM.

Over a cup of steaming-hot coffee, I discussed the migrant movement with father and son. They were curious to know how the whole movement had started and how I as an individual had managed to make this kind of brisk progress with sending people home. They asked me what kind of machinery and infrastructure I had, as I had achieved so much in so short a while. Both Uddhavji and Aaditya told me that if I required any assistance, the Maharashtra government would be happy to help.

I also met Bhagat Singh Koshyari, the governor of Maharashtra, over a cup of tea. He invited me to Raj Bhavan and congratulated me for my efforts in helping migrant workers return home. He also wanted to give me a note of appreciation for the work I had done.

My interactions were brief and cut across party lines. One of the first political leaders to call me was Priyanka Gandhi Vadra. She spoke to me for around ten minutes. Over the call, she conveyed to me that she was impressed by the kind of work I had done and the results achieved. Priyanka said, 'Sonu, you deserve huge congratulations. You will become a household name for the work you have done. If you need any kind of assistance in any part of India, I am just a phone call away.'

I also got a nickname from the chief minister of Punjab, Captain Amarinder Singh. Singh Sa'ab is someone I have known for a long time. I usually try and see him (if his schedule permits) on my trips to Punjab. Over the years, he has kept himself updated on my efforts to do social work in and around Moga. He nicknamed me 'Moga Boy' on his social media handle. On 28 May, Captain Sa'ab tweeted, 'It fills me with immense pride whenever I read about my fellow Punjabis going beyond their call of duty to help those in need and this time it is our Moga boy @SonuSood who has been actively helping migrant workers by arranging for their food and transportation. Good work Sonu!'

Mission beyond Migrants

It began with migrants from Mumbai, but as the 'get in touch with Sonu Sood' message gave momentum to the movement,

I found myself forsaking sleep and family time to arrange the airlifting of the helpless from all corners of the world, even from as far as Australia and Kyrgyzstan. It was no longer only about migrant workers.

In June, I received a complicated request from two boys in Australia. They said that they were stuck there and wanted to find a way back to India. They had to perform the last rites of their father, so they couldn't afford to observe the fourteen-day quarantine before the funeral. I got them the required permissions from Delhi, and they could fly back to India. One of the boys was from Odisha and the other from Madhya Pradesh. It was so heart-warming to be able to help someone through an emotional crisis. I knew how important it was for a family to be together when they had lost an elder.

In July, 4000 students were stranded in Kyrgyzstan and were unable to find a safe passage to India. When I got a distress message from them and we swung into action, it was another complex situation. The process involved speaking to authorities in the PMO, the Kyrgyzstan embassy and, of course, the Indian embassy in Kyrgyzstan. We also needed a whole range of other permissions, because of the sensitive times we are in. At first glance, bringing back such a large contingent of students looked like an impossibly heavy load to carry. But you will it and the way opens up. What started near a traffic signal in Kalwa had spread, as if on wings, to Kyrgyzstan.

In one of the following chapters, I've shared with you how we accomplished the daunting task of coordinating with and carrying home a spectrum of international evacuees, including students, labourers and medical-emergency patients from different parts of the world.

One of our worries was that with the success and the impact of the movement, we couldn't always focus solely on the mission or give undivided attention to rescuing people. My attention, and that of the team, was diverted to the nuisance of touts who had sprung up to feed off the miseries of migrant workers. We began to hear about touts even in Mumbai who had jumped in to collect money from unsuspecting poor people. The bloodsuckers went around telling the stranded, 'Pay us X amount and we'll put you on the transport provided by Sonu Sood.'

As it often happens in a project so vast, a few people did get conned, but when I learnt about this, we found a way to block such frauds. But it added to our work, as authentication of each and every passenger became a mandatory part of the process. The team would send messages that gave each individual the details and timings of the train or bus that he or she would be travelling in. There was an 'SS' (Sonu Sood) barcode devised! We had to be on high alert to ensure that no one was misusing my name.

We had to beef up our security too, because messages sometimes turned into rumours. For instance, when I was organizing a trainload of about 1200 people for Jaunpur, word spread that Sonu Sood's special train was ready to leave from Palghar. When I reached Vasai, I found approximately 4000 people thronging the place. I could foresee a law-and-order problem in the midst of the pandemic. The situation got out of hand, as there were wailing children, heartbroken elders and unreasonable people too in that crowd. It was almost impossible for me to let only 1200 people board the train. After the train departed, I sent the others to various shelters, including my own hotel in Juhu. Two days later, I was able to organize a large fleet of buses to take the rest of them to their homes. Fortunately, this chapter, too, ended happily, without any casualties or untoward incidents.

When the Indian Institute of Human Brands (IIHB) interviewed 110 corporate customers and reached out to 550 consumers to rate the performance of celebrities during the lockdown, I was astonished to find my name at the top of the heap, with respected seniors Akshay Kumar and Amitabh Bachchan at the second and third positions. How did I, hitherto known as the 6-foot-3-inch superstar with six-pack abs and two sharp dimples, reach there?

Where it started and what proportions it reached is something I'm still trying to fathom. I'm humbled. But of one thing I'm certain. Who I am today had its beginnings in the family into which I was born. That's where the Moga Boy was weaned on values that sustained him and brought him this far.

'A father's goodness is higher than the mountain. A mother's goodness deeper than the sea,' goes a Japanese proverb.

I was born in Patiala, but Moga, today a three-hour drive from my birthplace, was where I grew up. Moga was always special; Moga was home.

It unfailingly delights me to be identified as the 'Moga Boy'. I went to Sacred Heart School and Dayanand Mathra Dass College, better known as D.M. College, in Moga, and I was incredibly proud that my great-granddad and my granddad were patrons of many educational institutions there. They were known for their widespread charity work, and it swelled my chest with pride to know that many of the schools and colleges in Moga were built on land that belonged to our family.

I am told that when I was born, a telegram was sent to my father in Moga, saying that a son had arrived in their lives. When he drove down to Patiala to see me, my mother's family greeted him with, '*Badhai ho, aapke ghar mein kulcha paida hua hai* (Congratulations, a kulcha has been born in your family).' Family lore has it that I was so round and chubby that I resembled a kulcha, the fat stuffed roti so relished in our region. To link everything with wholesome food is typically Punjabi. To this day, my cousins in Punjab and Delhi call me Kulcha.

Mixed into this quintessential Punjabi ambience was a very fine non-traditional reality. 'Black Lives Matter' and 'All Lives Matter' are millennial slogans, but similar values were inculcated in me in childhood, particularly the idea of gender equality. The *puttar,* the male offspring, may be a big deal in all Punjabi households, and I was too. But sandwiched as I was between two sisters and that rare phenomenon, a working mother, absolute equality was the unstated thumb rule in my family.

I've heard the saying, 'Children are great imitators, so give them something great to imitate.' My parents sure did that. When they got married, my mom, Saroj Sood, landed a job as a professor at D.M. College, one of the oldest and most respected institutions in Moga since the 1920s. She taught English and history, and I still remember the time her salary was only Rs 440. However, the prestige attached to her work as an educationist made people respect our family even more than before. I was so incredibly proud of her that I would take her to college pillion riding with me on my Bajaj Chetak scooter. After my classes got over, I would wait for her to finish hers and ride home with her. I can't describe how grand it felt, having your parent as a teacher.

We revelled in the reputation of being an educated family and it brought us a lot of attention and, if I may say so, even reflected glory. Education has its own merits. So, values like gender equality, respect for working women and a premium on education were all around me and became a part of me. At the beginning of my parents' marriage, my mother was a great financial support to the family. Though Dad had a shop, it was, quite clearly, her steady income that helped us afford a decent lifestyle. For sure, this was unusual for that time and brought with it its share of social barbs. Some were slightly sceptical, even critical, of this unconventional 'educated-*bahu*-bringing-home-money' arrangement. However, my parents were comfortable with each other, and there was healthy mutual respect, love and understanding between them.

Looking back, I realize how much both of them invested in this relationship. On her part, Mom never brought her financial independence into their equation. And on his part, Dad never let the 'what will people think' syndrome worry either of them. All of this subconsciously seeped into me, as it would have into any child I guess.

Mom worked equally hard at being a homemaker. For my sisters and me, having both parents working meant that we realized the value of discipline, dogged hard work and money early in life; it all got naturally ingrained in us. We saw and understood from a young age that in some homes both parents held on to jobs to keep the kitchen fires burning. And it wasn't as if Mom worked only for the salary. She gave it her all. In fact, as events proved later, she gave it her life.

But it wasn't a case of all work and no play. Ours was a joyful family, where happily, all our childish demands were met. Be it a bicycle, a skipping rope or a cricket kit—there were no PlayStations in those days—we got it all. But we also learnt to value it all. As I grew out of my teens, I would sometimes feel that maybe I had been too demanding and that my parents might have had to dig deep into their pockets, even deny themselves something, to buy me all that I asked for. But I consider this sort of guilt-tripping positive, as it helps you appreciate all that life has offered you and keeps you balanced.

My father had a shop called Bombay Cloth House in Moga. He passed away on 7 February 2016, but the shop still stands. I've been running it for sentimental reasons, with the same staff that he worked with. My father also loved people and was in his element feeding everybody around. He urged me to always keep an open house. The Punjabi custom of langar (feeding large groups) was practised at home. Even after I achieved stardom, Dad often expected me to open my house to strangers for a meal. For him, the true measure of a successful man lay in how many mouths he fed. Fortunately for me, my wife, Sonali, also resonates with this thought. It is because of such similar traits between us that I often think that Sonali is a life partner and soulmate.

I often wonder how my parents did it. They not only worked hard and were attentive as parents, but they also had space in their hearts and in their busy schedules for people unrelated to us. I therefore believe that if they could, anybody can.

'For it is in giving that we receive.' It could well have been Saroj Sood, the professor of English and history, mouthing this wisdom to me, her son, and not St Francis of Assisi.

My parents led by example. My father was more reserved and less vocal. My mother, by virtue of being a teacher, was always articulate. I grew up watching her give free tuitions to a lot of her underprivileged students. In fact, if a less fortunate student missed their studies because housework kept them away from classes, my mother would make me drive her to their homes where she would personally cajole the elders and make them understand the importance of education. She would make them aware that they as parents had to give their children the time and indulgence needed for education.

My mother and father treated Monika Sood (Sharma), aka Mona, older than me by a year and a half, and me on par. In turn, Mona and I tended to pamper and practically parent my younger sister, Malvika Sood (Sachar), Gunu to us, who was ten years younger than me. Mona and I were so close that we even went to school together. With no gender discrimination at home between girls and boys, I got no extra privileges as the 'only son' of the house.

On the contrary, more than the puttar, it was Mona who was the family favourite, because she was both exceptionally bright and an obedient daughter. A scientist in Washington today, Mona was a consistent school and college topper. Woman power was thus an intrinsic part of my life.

Ten thousand hours. That was the golden cut-off that Malcolm Gladwell wrote about in his outstanding bestseller *Outliers*. Those who touched the pinnacle in the arts, sports or indeed any field were separated by 10,000 hours from those who were gifted but did not ace it. Gladwell's research concluded that it was 10,000 hours of dedicated practice that turned talent into gold.

I can neither claim to have touched the pinnacle nor have I kept count of the hours. But all through life, whether in my studies or in chasing my impossible dream of becoming an actor in Mumbai or in pulling off the gargantuan Ghar Bhejo movement, I seem to have been guided by an instinct to put in that kind of slog at every turn.

My life is a textbook example of hard work and never giving up.

Mona was the benchmark before me. She scored a consistent 90 per cent in every class she went to. I was nowhere near her brilliance, but not wanting to ever let my parents down, I made up for not being as good as Mona by putting far more effort into my studies. That helped me take my score to 75–80 per cent, but my mother would push me to do better. She would tell me, '*Beta*, I'm a professor. I have tutored many bright students. You need to up the ante and pass with flying colours.' I had to live up to the standards set by Mona.

However, my parents didn't pressure us to perform. We were encouraged to study well but never pulled up, spanked or harshly scolded. The life lesson I got was the importance of perseverance and the steely quality of not calling it quits. These are qualities that have been my companions all through life as an adult and as a professional. They helped me as an actor, and they rushed to my aid during the Ghar Bhejo movement.

Having someone like Mona to look up to didn't demoralize me. Instead, it goaded me into pushing my limits further and further. That spirit of perseverance, of never giving up, came with me to Mumbai when I arrived with no connections, no recommendations. All I had was my height, my physique, Rs 5500 in my pocket and my grit.

That spirit is also what drove me to meet what seemed like the insurmountable challenge posed by the Ghar Bhejo movement.

My siblings and I have always shared a strong bond, and all through her life, my mother believed that long after she and my father were gone, 'Sonu will look after his two sisters'. This belief did not have its roots in gender superiority or in the male child being stronger or better equipped than his sisters. It had to do with the native, natural instinct of protectiveness that I had in me, and one doesn't have to quell that just to prove a point about the equality of genders.

Twice a year, on Raksha Bandhan and on Bhai Dooj, my mother would tell me, 'As their brother, you should always care for your sisters, protect them and make them feel special.' I can't deny that even today I feel a surge of protectiveness that comes from somewhere deep within for my sisters. It's not about being the alpha male; it's like instinctively caring for your wife and your children. It's an innate trait that's honed by parents in all Indian homes.

To me, it's the emotional quotient of a man that makes him caring and protective. You don't have to fight it because it does not negate gender equality. In fact, nurturing this instinct helped me channel the right sentiments during the coronavirus pandemic. It was this need, this urge, this feeling to want to protect that drove me. The beneficiaries of my protectiveness were in no way related to me. They were simply people who brought out compassion in me.

Early lessons imparted by my parents thus made me the man I am today. Mom's quest in life was simple. She wanted to tutor as many children as she could. Today, when I learn about an Anand Kumar who coached underprivileged children in Patna, Bihar, or about the numerous coaching tutors in Kota, Rajasthan, who provide extra lessons to countless students each year, I think of my mother. She, too, was a committed educationist.

Mom felt so strongly about education that she wanted to teach as many children as she could, especially those from economically challenged families who could not afford tuitions or extra coaching. Even today, I am filled with a sense of pride that this was who my mother was. A wave of sadness also engulfs me, because she put education, her purpose in life, before herself. I wish she had taken care of herself and paid more attention to her health. But she did what she did because education was her calling. Her life has been an example of selflessness for me. As they say, it's your parents who are often your gurus, philosophers and guides.

When you are the son of a professor and the brother of a school topper, you raise the bar for yourself. The importance of good grades was never lost on me, and my constant endeavour was to put in peak performance at whatever I chose to do. My mother didn't want me to sit at Dad's shop. She wanted me to stand tall, literally and metaphorically. She always dreamt of making me an engineer, which was why I headed to YCCE, Nagpur.

Terrorism was at its peak in Punjab back then. Therefore, many of us, especially the boys, moved out and either went overseas or to universities in other Indian states. I think Nagpur beckoned me, as that was where I met my wife, P. Sonali, and it was there, in my second year of engineering, that the acting bug first bit me.

Sonali and I both took part in a fashion show in the city. Right there on the ramp, I was hit by the desire to be a model, and I also met Sonali for the first time. The daughter of a well-respected banker, she belonged to a Telugu family settled in Nagpur. She was doing a degree in mass communication.

At one of our early meetings, I proposed marriage to Sonali. It was my way of assuring her that I was serious about her, that my intentions were honourable. I told her how much I wanted a girl like her in my life. To be by my side, Sonali enrolled in an MBA course, which gave her two additional years of student life in Nagpur.

With educated parents on both sides, the north–south issue never cropped up in her family or mine. There was harmonious cultural inclusiveness with Sonali in my life. While my mother's sole grouse was that I didn't tell her about my relationship with Sonali early enough, everybody in my family took to Sonali easily because she was, and is, such a warm girl. Sonali even attended my elder sister's wedding in Delhi. So she was a part of my life long before she actually became my *woti* (wife) on 28 December 2000.

Sonali knew about my secret dream, which lay far away from the world of engineering. But it was only after I got my degree that I gingerly broached the subject of a career in showbiz with my parents. I braced myself to hear them say, 'Why would you want to start a struggle all over again when you are a qualified engineer?' However, both of them had only one piece of advice for me: 'Go chase your dream, make sure you succeed, don't give up midway. Give it your best shot.'

'Life begins at the end of your comfort zone,' according to Neale Donald Walsch, author of *Conversations with God*. For a student in the midst of a tough engineering degree course, to wake up one day and say 'I want to become a Hindi film actor' bordered on lunacy. Let me repeat this:

'It's impossible,' said Pride
'It's risky,' said Experience
'It's pointless,' said Reason
'Give it a try,' whispered the Heart

When I stepped out of the comfort zone of a steady future as a qualified engineer, the only wind under my wings was the unwavering support of my parents, who told me, 'Go for it, son.' My battles with rejection, humiliation and the ensuing dejection were motivational milestones in my journey and played a big part in the making of the celebrity face Sonu Sood. But becoming famous was not, as I had imagined, the end goal of my life. This celebrity face was imperative for the Ghar Bhejo movement to succeed, for doors to open and make things happen. That was the grand plan of the powers up there which unfolded before me in 2020.

There were many inspirational notes engraved on every milestone from Moga to Mumbai. Thomas Jefferson's words still resonate with me: 'If you want something you've never had, you must be willing to do something you've never done.'

Before embarking on my Mumbai sojourn, I made Delhi my starting point. It was closer home, and with cousins there, it was a more familiar terrain. My parents offered me money, but I felt I had to go through the grind myself. Only then would I have a winning story to tell.

At the end of six months, I had barely earned Rs 5500; eleven bills of Rs 500 each. I still remember the denomination because that money was so precious. When I had only Rs 5500 left in my pocket, I headed for my dream destination—Mumbai. I had a bike, which I shipped earlier by a freight train, and the next day I took the Golden Temple Mail without even a reserved seat.

I was twenty-five years old and brimming with the excitement of a journey into the unknown. It didn't scare me; instead, it spurred me on, irrespective of the hurdles and stumbles, the disillusionment and discouragement. When I spread a newspaper in the passage close to a smelly toilet on the train, I experienced the adrenaline rush of an adventure more than the spectre of despondent failure.

I bribed the ticket collector with Rs 150 so he'd let me curl up in the corridor, where passengers heading to and returning from the toilet would wake me up intermittently and a cold, sharp breeze blowing in from under the compartment door would go right into my head. I had no blanket to cover myself, but the eagerness of following my dream had numbed all my senses.

The motivating factor in such an impossible chase has to be your own optimistic anticipation of achievement and disregard for the demoralizing advice of anybody else. For me, that first hint of a dampener came right there on the train to Mumbai, from a man seated near me in the corridor who noted my clothes and rightly sized me up as a wannabe actor. He told me, 'Don't get your hopes up. In Mumbai, outsiders barely get a chance. Unless you have a godfather, the chances of making it in films are slim.' He told me that he had himself tried and failed, and was now going to Mumbai only to pack up and return to Punjab. But he didn't succeed in disheartening me, for I wanted to work out my own destiny.

I had been to Mumbai before I landed here on my star trek, but my knowledge of the city was close to a cipher. I knew it was home to renowned actors like Dharmendra, Amitabh Bachchan and Vinod Khanna. I knew it had a Film City. And I knew there was a station called Bandra. I was also hopeful that if you roamed the streets of Mumbai, some film-maker would notice you and may actually cast you in one of his movies.

I stood outside Film City and gazed longingly at it. But I couldn't put a foot inside until I had handed bribe money of Rs 400 to the security guard. I remember taunting him, 'One day I will be an actor, and you will be saluting me. And today you are asking for my hard-earned 400 bucks?' He cheekily replied, 'Sir, when you become an actor, I will salute you. But today, you have to give me 400, or I'm not going to let you inside.'

I thus gained entry to roam around the studio. I stood outside the sets, optimistic that my 6' 3" height and my chiselled physique would draw the attention of some director, who would give me a role in his film.

When you're clueless, there are advisers aplenty hovering around you. It's up to you to sift the well-meaning from the wastrels and accept that mistakes will be made. But that shouldn't deter you. One guy said I needed to register with the Cine and TV Artistes' Association and get myself a card. There were so many suggestions coming from everywhere that I didn't know what to believe. I was practical, so I bought a film directory that had the names and numbers of production companies and advertising agencies.

My instinctive skill was in making a to-do plan for each day. I would make a shortlist, put it in my pocket and tell myself that these were the offices I would visit today to hand over my portfolio photographs in person and request an audition. It was tough going with no godfather, no filmland connections. I would walk miles, visiting various production offices. I had my bike, but not enough money to buy fuel.

I had a monthly pass from Borivali to Churchgate, and the Mumbai local became my best friend. I would get off at stations like Khar, Mahalaxmi and Elphinstone Road and make my way to film offices to drop off a set of fresh pictures or check if they'd found something suitable for me. Advertising agencies in Churchgate, Everest Building in Tardeo, Maker Chambers in Nariman Point and some offices in and around Bandra became regular haunts. I was on this beat, unflagging, for months on end.

Franklin D. Roosevelt: 'A smooth sea never made a skilled sailor.' It was a turbulent ride to fame and fortune for me, often disappointing and demeaning. I could never come face to face with any producer or director of consequence. I could go only as far as their first or second assistants.

I was so guileless and ignorant that I didn't know B- and C-grade movies also existed. I would spot a film poster in some random window, walk in and ask for a role. Sometimes, I would trudge for miles only to find that the address I had was fake.

It was only too human to feel defeated, deflated and dejected at times, but after a good night's sleep, I'd be back on the beat, rebooted and raring to go.

On the days that I took the bike out, I felt heroic. I had my own wheels and didn't have to use public transport. But a bike ride had its own challenges. When I'd reach south Mumbai all the way from Andheri, where I had my PG (paying guest) digs, I'd be dishevelled and tanned. There had to be a quick detour to the studio washroom to freshen up, but I guess I wasn't at my presentable best because work eluded me.

At one of the offices I visited at Famous Studios in Mahalaxmi, the receptionist refused to even look in my direction. She was so indifferent that she gestured at me to place the envelope on the counter and leave. I remember it because it was a real low finding that someone didn't have the courtesy to even look up at me and speak. At this rate, how would I ever catch anybody's attention? I counselled myself and repeated, 'One day, you'll not just be noticed but will reach a position where this same receptionist at Famous Studios will stop what she's doing to give you her full attention.'

A desperate situation calls for desperate measures, and one was always thinking of how to draw attention. Standing in that office and feeling helpless, I came up with the idea that if I asked her for a glass of water, the receptionist would have to look up. I did just that, and I was asked to take a seat and offered a glass of water. Of course, I also hoped that as she looked up, she would check me out and note my height and physique. Then maybe, just maybe, I could land at least an audition. It didn't pan out that way, but that became my act of the day—giving my pictures and asking for a glass of water. I went to about thirty offices and repeated the trick. Before I knew it, I had drunk thirty glasses of water and my bladder was ready to burst.

Incidentally, I had the misconception that I was a fashionable, natty dresser. For a boy from Moga via Nagpur, I had a decent dress sense and in college, I used to be much complimented for my sartorial choices. However, in Mumbai, I realized that I was a part of the crowd. Out here, everyone had a style, and most people had access to smart and trendy wardrobes. Also, my struggle had taken a certain percentage of my flair out of me.

Albert Camus: 'In the depth of winter, I finally learned that within me there lay an invincible summer.' Every time disillusionment loomed before me, I told myself that God up there was watching my struggle and would reward me with success. I had an incalculable amount of faith in myself, the belief that I would pull it off no matter how rough the ride was going to be. I also believed in the power of the Supreme.

An additional quality that never deserted me was my sincerity. The journeys on the local train, the treks on foot from the Mahalaxmi station to Famous Studios, the receptionists not even looking up to see who was handing over his pictures—nothing dashed my hopes.

If anybody out there harbours the kind of dream I had, my one-line advice would be, 'The struggle in Mumbai is like holding your breath underwater. It's an endurance test. The longer you hold your breath, the longer you'll last.' To go through a struggle in the film industry, you must be prepared to endure unimaginable rejection. If you are fortunate like I was, you may get a chance to put your head out of the water within a year or two. Sometimes, it may take a decade to be seen or noticed. Please be patient. Patience is the mother of all virtues. Your patience will be tested at every juncture. You have to grin and bear it. If you don't have it in you to hold your breath for an indeterminate period, find an alternative career; don't waste your life.

My father and mother wrote letters to me to keep my spirits up, asking me to not give up. Mom wrote more frequently, sending me tips and poems to keep me charged. My parents' letters are still a prized possession. Unfortunately, both have passed on, but their neatly filed letters are still my go-to boosters.

I faced the usual pile of rejections and humiliations that aspiring actors face when they dare to land in Mumbai without a single letter of recommendation. But the more intense the insults, the deeper my determination to succeed. It's a simple choice before you—you can cringe at the humiliation, back off and go home empty-handed. Or you can just ignore it and go for the kill. There's a higher chance that if you do the latter, you may have something to show for your struggles.

The Rat Race

It sure was full of rats.

I relocated many times in Mumbai and the list of addresses is long. But one of the first was a place at RTO Lane in

Andheri where artiste coordinator Sushma Kaul rented out a one-bedroom apartment to four paying guests, all strugglers looking for their pot of gold in Hindi cinema. Sushmaji was an important part of that phase. She emitted a rare kindness. On some occasions, when I couldn't pay my rent on time, she would allow me to defer it without a tantrum. She also inquired about the well-being of her paying guests. At a time when life wasn't exactly a path strewn with roses, even this wee bit of compassion went a long way in making me feel that I mattered.

Ah, but she also had the rent-free mischief of rats in her apartment. The rodents scuttled across wires at night like trapeze artists. A couple of times, when I was just about to fall asleep, a fat one fell on me and made me shudder. Once, I walked out of the apartment, sat beside a bridge close by and called my parents. I told them I wasn't getting enough sleep. I didn't tell them about my rodent company, but parents are intuitive.

During one such call, my mother read out these lines from a Robert Frost poem to me:

The woods are lovely, dark and deep,
But I have promises to keep,
And miles to go before I sleep,
And miles to go before I sleep.

My Mr India Moment

My bike had been spluttering every couple of days. It was my only prized possession when I first arrived in Mumbai from Delhi, and it developed a snag when it was offloaded at the

Mumbai Central station. Out of the Rs 5500 that I had in my pocket, I had to shell out Rs 3000 to make it roadworthy again, which left me with virtually nothing for my stay and struggle.

An icy feeling of defeat was creeping in, and I wrestled with the temptation of asking my parents for money when I got a call from Far Video, an advertising firm that belonged to Jeet and Kailash Surendranath. They wanted me for a commercial for Action Shoes, and I was going to be paid Rs 3000 a day for three days. This was the sign from the universe that men like Paulo Coelho had written about—signals that told me that whatever I endured would one day be rewarded. But at that moment, all I felt was a load being taken off me. I exhaled with relief that I would soon have Rs 9000 to see me through the next few weeks.

Though I was riding my bike, it felt as if I was walking on air as I rushed to Film City for the shoot, where this time, I didn't have to bribe anybody to gain entry. Yes, I'd become a model for Action Shoes. But I came down to earth soon enough when I found twenty other equally tall guys hanging around. My sense of self-importance got further deflated on realizing that I was going to be in the background, in the role of a drum player. Also, they packed me off in two days instead of three, and I panicked because I thought I would be losing the Rs 3000 for the third day. But I got the full payment of Rs 9000, which was a huge relief. Still, more dejection was in store. When the ad finally came out, I hadn't even made it to the final cut. I had vanished; I was invisible, like Mr India.

'Hope lies in dreams, in imagination, and in the courage of those who dare to turn dreams into reality.' Virologist

Jonas Salk uttered that in his quest for a vaccine, but it is applicable in any trying situation. One such spark of hope sprang up when I was at Bana's Gym in Four Bungalows, Andheri, for my evening workout routine. I got a message on my pager, inviting me for an audition for a part in a Shah Rukh Khan film. I rode to Film City on my bike and was exhilarated to find myself on the sets of Mansoor Khan's *Josh*. They had recreated Goa there, and its magnificent scale took my breath away. After making us hang around for forty-odd minutes, the artiste coordinator deigned to call us. We were about twenty-five eager young men waiting for the magic to happen, but the assistant director didn't find any of us worthy of even an audition and we were packed off without much ado.

I had rushed out of the gym and ridden like I was in a bike rally to reach Film City at night, only to be waved away like a housefly. But I bashed on regardless.

In any sort of struggle, physical fitness provides the fuel to keep one moving forward on the toughest terrain. Like everything else in life, I pushed and strove, and became a fitness freak. Even as a student of engineering, I would hit the gym with a vengeance in Nagpur. I have always loved that part of the day when I work out.

I met Satyajeet Chaurasia, or Satya—now a celebrity fitness instructor—for the first time in Nagpur. When I was staying at Adarsh Nagar as a paying guest, Satya and Devashish (also a friend) had come to Mumbai from Nagpur, and they stayed with me at my PG digs. I'm the one who actually went around with Satya and helped him find a place to open his gym. I went with him to actors like Saif Ali Khan, asking them to come over to Barbarian Gym to work out. I was naturally a regular at Barbarian, where Satya encouraged me to work harder on my physique, and before I knew it, the story of my six-pack abs began to circulate.

Chennai Express

Fortunately for me, I didn't have too much time to sulk or feel sorry for myself. Around December 1996, about six months after coming to Mumbai, I got a message on my pager, asking me to come to Chennai. I had no clue that this was going to be my express ticket to fame and fortune, for around the corner was my big break in superstar Vijayakanth's Tamil film *Kallazhagar* (1999).

I took the train to Chennai, unsure of entering a territory I knew nothing about. My coordinator and friend M.J. Ramanan, who is also a film director today, met me at the Chennai Central station to take me on his Bullet to Vijaya Vauhini Studios. Ramanan was one of the first casting guys to spot me in Mumbai. He had met my Mumbai agent, Sushma Kaul (also my landlady), and she had passed him a photograph of mine. Ramanan was impressed with my physical attributes and told Sushmaji that she should send me to Chennai for a role opposite Vijayakanth Sir. He enlightened me on how fortuitous this was for me. He was of the belief that whoever got cast as the antagonist opposite Vijayakanth usually became a household name. Vijayakanth Sir was considered a lucky mascot for actors being launched in a negative role. And that certainly came true for me.

When we reached the studio, I was dressed in a white T-shirt and military-green cargos. Henry, the producer, guided me to the make-up room and took me to a high chair, the typical ones where artistes sit and do their make-up. But before anybody could touch my face, I had to pass a test. The producer and director asked me to remove my T-shirt and show them my physique. I passed with flying colours, and my make-up session began.

I was paid Rs 50,000 for eight months of my time. I had to shave my head and then grow my hair back. It upset my coordinator, Ramanan, who told me that I had sold myself at a discount. He told me that I could have easily demanded and got Rs 3 lakh. However, I was so insecure about losing whatever little I was getting that I didn't even think of negotiating the fee.

I went back and forth between the studio and the guest house on the local casting guy Natraj's Luna, which was an uncomfortable ride for a six-footer, but it was the only transport available to me. At the guest house, the producer stressed on the fact that I was being given an air-conditioned room. 'A/C room, sir,' he said, to emphasize what a privilege it was.

I had come from Moga to Mumbai, earmarking Hindi films as my goal. But while eyeing the main door, one shouldn't miss the other windows of opportunity that may open out of the blue. If I hadn't gone through those unexpected windows, I would not have lived to tell the unbelievable tale of the Punjabi boy who got his introduction to fame and fortune through a culture and language quite unknown to him. Tamil, Telugu, Kannada—I didn't know a word of any of these languages, or indeed the societal mores of the states where these are spoken.

My belief has always been, 'The difference between who you are and who you want to be is what you do.'

I tried to learn those languages and, characteristically, gave them my all. If Punjabi and Hindi had to be topped with seemingly tongue-twisting dialogues in Tamil and Telugu to help move towards my dream, I was ready for that and enthusiastic about learning new survival skills. If parathas and pure ghee had to be temporarily replaced with a diet of idli-sambar and dosa for the dream to fructify into an achievement, I was game. I did what tennis ace Arthur Ashe advised: 'Start where you are. Use what you have. Do what you can.'

Eventually, I got stardom via Chennai, Bengaluru and Hyderabad. Idli-sambar and dosa became my staple food because, as predicted by Ramanan, my career took off like a rocket after my super-hit debut with Vijayakanth. I was flooded with offers in Telugu, Tamil and Kannada movies. And fortune smiled at me abundantly.

Mouthing dialogues in Tamil and Telugu was a huge assignment, even if they had to be later dubbed by someone else. I had to memorize my lines and deliver them with the right facial expressions and body language during the shot. My ability to swot up for my exams and sweat it out to get those six-pack abs, in short, to slog it out whatever the odds, stayed with me like a loyal companion. I was so determined to succeed that I would have taken a shot at learning even the most difficult language under the sun, because that was what had I set myself up for.

One of the factors that worked for me was that a north Indian in south India is generally treated with patience and kindness. Cue cards in Roman English were provided and assistant directors were helpful. Language barriers were thus crossed through the generosity of my colleagues and my own disposition of never giving up.

People may think it dramatic and label it an exaggeration if I were to draw a parallel between me and those migrants who had set off on foot. But there were days when my meagre allowances and the desire to save what I could urged me to walk miles to reach the studios down south. Eternally looking for a silver lining, I would take it as a fitness challenge and hit the roads. I did this especially during the evenings when I didn't have to worry about arriving drenched in sweat at my destination. I'd just set off on foot from the studio to my guest house or hotel.

Tere Mere Beach Mein

I'd landed the plum role of the mean main villain with a shaven head in *Kallazhagar* because of my height and my six-pack abs. But it was an embarrassing discovery that I wasn't equipped to pull off a fight scene, such an essential for the kind of villain I was playing.

I could take the punches that life had been landing on me. But during my first fight sequence with Vijayakanth Sir, he realized that I didn't know how to take punches before the camera or give the right reactions. Once again, their patience and my determination combined and paid off, as he asked the producer to give me a month's training in how to duck and punch and give the right facial expressions. I was red-faced and contrite that because of me the fights could only be filmed after a month.

I became a regular at one of the most famous beaches in Asia, the Marina Beach in Chennai, where the action coordinator put me through my paces and taught me all the required stunts. I was also asked to 'look like a villain'. So, a special assistant was assigned to me, only to ensure that I ate more and bulked up.

After a month of sweat and blood that went into my rigorous training, I was ready to face Vijayakanth Sir in the climax fight of *Kallazhagar*. When the climax of this film became one of the most talked-about sequences of its time, it felt as euphoric as holding aloft the Champion's Trophy or standing first in university. The film set the box office ablaze.

Work and wealth poured in from the south, but I still yearned for the door to Hindi cinema to open for me. And it did. With one foot still firmly in the south, I made my way into Hindi films. Gurdas Maan's *Zindagi Khoobsoorat Hai* (2002); *Shaheed-e-Azam* (2002), where I got to play the legendary role of Bhagat Singh; and Mani Ratnam's *Yuva* (2004) came my way. But I also had to accept lesser roles, in films like *Divorce: Not Between Husband and Wife* (2005) and *Aashiq Banaya Aapne* (2005). Life in films is always very tumultuous: you take what you get. For those who think superstars have it easy, I'd like to point out how far that is from reality. You get to do some great stuff alongside the insignificant, but the motto here is to keep doing it right. My introductory films were a mixed bunch, but my patience saw me graduate to blockbusters. Movies like *Singh Is Kinng*, *Dabangg* and *Happy New Year* ushered me into A-grade commercial cinema.

My earnings in the south and some money that I'd borrowed from my parents helped me buy my first piece of property in Mumbai. I bought Urmila Matondkar's sixth-floor apartment in a building called Casablanca in Andheri. She was on top of her game then, and I got a kick out of saying that I now owned her apartment.

I paid Rs 31 lakh for that three-bedroom flat but scrambled and failed to put together an additional Rs 25,000 for the garage. Her father wouldn't wait and sold the parking space to someone else. Later on, I bought two more flats in Casablanca on the fourth floor. That's where I reside now. The sixth-floor flat is still mine, but to this day, that parking space could never be mine.

Like my professional life, where the south and the north merged, my personal life too made me a multicultural man as Sonali and I got married long before I gained a foothold in Hindi cinema. But just when life seems set and you've steadied your stance, a blow comes from nowhere to unbalance you.

I had signed *Singh Is Kinng*, a big Hindi film, and was feeling like Sonu Sood is King when my mother fell seriously ill. My mother was as industrious as an ant. On icy winter mornings, when the temperature would drop to as low as 2 degrees centigrade in Moga, and the thought of leaving the comfort of our blankets would make us shiver, Mom would be ready at 5.30 a.m. to receive her first batch of students for tuitions.

She taught them till around 8.30 a.m., then made breakfast for all of us. After this, she'd be off to college for her lectures. In the evenings, she would once again be teaching another bunch of students. Her days were long, and to me, they seemed endless. I emphasize her punishing schedule because somewhere between all these coaching lessons, her

throat started to tire. Doctors advised her to slow down and
rest her throat, but my mother didn't pay heed to them. She
felt teaching was her *pehla dharam,* her religious duty.

She continued to strain herself even after she was
diagnosed with interstitial lung disease (ILD), a condition
which scars the lung tissue. It eventually leads to the lungs
working at 30 per cent capacity, and since there isn't enough
oxygen in the bloodstream, an ILD patient feels fatigued and
breathless. With constant speaking and tutoring, my mother's
condition deteriorated.

Once, when she visited me in Mumbai, I took her
on my Hero Honda bike to Asian Heart Institute at
the Bandra–Kurla Complex, where they directed me to
Dr Ashok Mahashur, the pulmonologist at Hinduja Hospital.
Dr Mahashur told us that her condition was not alarming,
and that if she continued to have her medication regularly,
she would be able to maintain status quo on her health for a
long time.

I would get very upset every time Mama had a severe
coughing fit and would tell Dr Mahashur that whatever the
expense, all I wanted was for her to recover. I took my parents
to the United States as well to consult doctors. I took her to
doctors in Washington, Houston and New York, to see as
many specialists as we could and get her the best treatment
available in this world. My mother would often call me
shravan-putra. She believed I was like Shravan Kumar from
the Ramayana who ferried his blind parents around in two
baskets that were placed on his shoulders. For my part, all I
wanted was Aladdin's magic lamp and a genie to make Mom
well again.

I have a strange observation to make about this kind of desperation where you hope against hope for a miracle. It brings a certain tenacity to your character and makes you the stronger for it. It's odd how a situation like this plays out.

My mother passed away on 13 October 2007, but till the very end, my efforts to restore her health continued untiringly.

Flashback to 13 October 2007. Around 6.30 a.m., when I got a call from my younger sister and she only sobbed over the phone, I knew something was wrong. Later, one of our caretakers, Ramu, called up to reconfirm my worst fears. Sonali was away in Nagpur, visiting her parents, and my older son, Eshaan, who was barely five years old, was asleep. I didn't know how I was going to make it to Moga. The journey seemed never-ending, and when I finally arrived, I was completely distraught.

I had already got my fair share of recognition by 2007. People recognized me at Mumbai airport and, as the public generally does, many of them clicked photographs too. I was wearing dark glasses to hide my tears, but there was a point when I was actually trembling. That's when some of them realized that something was seriously amiss. When I reached the mortuary in Moga and saw my mother's body, I broke down. I was so grief-stricken that I thought I wouldn't be able to go on with life. I honestly believed that this was the end for me. I was broken and defeated. I thought I would never be able to raise my head again.

I had signed *Singh Is Kinng* just before my mother passed away. But after her death, I went to my producer, Vipul Shah, and director, Anees Bazmee, and told them that I wanted to opt out of it as I wasn't in the right mental frame to work. Vipul and Anees were so caring that they waited for nearly a month for me to get my bearings.

I went to Australia to shoot for *Singh Is Kinng*, but even on the sets, I would have frequent meltdowns. The hurt was so deep, it was almost like a physical wound, palpable. I had lost my mojo. When I was alone, I worried that I would no longer be able to continue acting. I functioned like a robot, and the zeal to work went out of me.

'The song is ended but the melody lingers on,' as the American composer Irving Berlin has so beautifully summed up. It took me years to return to normality, but her melody continues to linger. As a character in drama series *The Wire* says, 'Ain't no shame in holding on to grief . . . as long as you make room for other things too.'

It also took me a while to realize that it was an irreparable loss for my father too. He, too, was ageing and I needed to be around for him, to make him proud of his son. I began to pick up the pieces and came back to the world of the living.

There is one more line that I would quote as an ode to my parents. 'You gave me a forever within the numbered days,' wrote John Green in *The Fault in Our Stars*. That's what my mother and father gave me. They gave me a forever.

And in this forever, let me share what a pregnant migrant woman, who had travelled home on one of our buses, did on reaching Jharkhand. She delivered a son and named him Sonu Sood Srivastava. Similarly, a plumber in Odisha, who reached home safely, opened a shop and put this up on the name board: Sonu Sood Welding Work Shop.

To think that when I entered showbiz I was asked to change my name! I was urged to rechristen myself with a fashionable moniker, like Aryan or Aryaman, because many felt that no one would take a name like Sonu Sood seriously.

It is ironical and a miracle that today, sons and shops are being given that very name. I say this with utter humility and conviction. When you believe in something, believe in it completely. Commit yourself to it. I believed in my name. To me, it was a blessing from my parents.

Whether movies, a movement or marriage, I am not commitment phobic. Try it, it works at every turn in life.

A tiny footnote to draw inspiration from:

Men Are from Mars, Women Are from Venus, says the book. For me, it was only about Venus. Not the planet, but Venus Records and Tapes in Juhu. It was a big production house. They had made *Baazigar* with Shah Rukh Khan and Kajol, *Josh* with Shah Rukh and Aishwarya Rai, *Badshah* with Shah Rukh and Twinkle Khanna, *Main Khiladi Tu Anari* with Akshay Kumar, Shilpa Shetty and Saif, *Akele Hum Akele Tum* with Aamir Khan and Manisha Koirala, and a dozen other major movies.

The Venus office was on my regular beat during my days of struggle. I had walked up and down that building, trying to catch the attention of the Jain brothers—who were the owners—for a break as an actor.

It was a break that never came. But here's a fun fact. Twenty years later, I became the proud owner of that very building in Juhu that once housed Venus Records and Tapes. I bought it, renovated it and, as a tribute to my father, named it Shakti Sagar Hotel.

I Am No Messiah is not a story of self-glorification. I was lucky, but many tenacious elements went into finding that luck. Like Lord Krishna said to Arjuna in the Mahabharat, a multitude of factors went into keeping Arjuna's chariot flying against Karna in battle. I concede that many extraneous forces shape our destinies, our paths. But what we need to help ourselves is resolve, an adherence to what we seek and sheer perseverance. My advice to everyone is: Go find your luck, go find your purpose. A pandemic is not reason enough to give up.

We have to learn to live with the vagaries of nature; we have to give up the old and make way for the new.

As it's often said, 'You can: end of story.'

If I can, you can, we can.

1

This One's for You, Mom

'1137. mails.
19000. fb messages.
4812. Insta messages.
6741. twitter messages.
Today's HELP messages.'

That's what I tweeted on 20 August 2020. That's the average number of messages I have been receiving every single day. That one tweet drew 10,477 comments on Twitter alone.

While it was unfeasible for me to personally respond to or act upon all of them, these messages were also the propellants that kept me on the fast track, steering me towards those who genuinely needed assistance and had to be extricated from a variety of situations.

It was through social media that I became aware of one such situation—a controversy that raged all through the months of July, August and a part of September 2020.

Every year, the National Testing Agency (NTA) organizes the National Eligibility-cum-Entrance Test for Undergraduates (NEET-UG), a single examination for students seeking admission into a medical or dental course (MBBS/BDS), and the Joint Entrance Examination (JEE) for engineering aspirants in India.

In September 2019, the NEET-UG became a common all-India entrance test for admission into medical colleges all over the country, including the All India Institute of Medical Sciences (AIIMS) and the Jawaharlal Institute of Postgraduate Medical Education and Research (JIPMER), which until recently used to conduct their own individual exams.

This single entrance test is for admissions into more than 66,000 MBBS and BDS seats across India. In 2018, approximately 80 per cent of the candidates wrote the NEET-UG in English, 11 per cent in Hindi, 4.31 per cent in Gujarati, 3 per cent in Bengali and 1.86 per cent in Tamil.

The JEE-Main, formerly the All India Engineering Entrance Examination (AIEEE), was introduced in 2002 and renamed in April 2013. This national-level competitive test is for admission into various undergraduate engineering and architecture courses, in institutes that accept the JEE-Main score, such as the National Institutes of Technology (NITs), the Indian Institutes of Information Technology (IIITs) and Government Funded Technical Institutes (GFTIs).

I am recounting these facts only to underscore the importance of these examinations for the students of aspirational India. Most students work hard over these exams, treating them as a lifeline to the future.

In 2020, the stressful year of the COVID-19 pandemic, over 8.58 lakh candidates registered for the JEE-Main and 15.97 lakh for the NEET. Generally, the JEE-Main exams are conducted in April, while the NEET-UG is held in May. However, due to the enforced lockdown this year, these vital exams were postponed twice. The NTA finally decided to hold the JEE-Main exams from 1–6 September and the NEET on 13 September. It led to a nationwide uproar.

Many cited the unprecedented complications that arose from the COVID-19 threat. Students from the flood-hit states of Bihar, Gujarat and Assam, from the downpour-drenched districts of Kerala and from regions with low Internet connectivity, like Jammu and Kashmir, had to grapple with more than the stress of the exams. For them, it was an additional struggle to appear for the exams. Lockdown orders, in varying degrees, were in place in 345 districts across the country. Given the drastic reduction in the number of operational public transport facilities, students in far-flung areas worried about how to reach the exam centres. Activists also pointed out that there was the very real risk of students travelling to different centres and returning home to multigenerational families and spreading the disease indiscriminately.

Students' organizations—such as the All India Students Association, Students' Federation of India and National Students' Union of India among others—held sustained social media campaigns to demand the cancellation or postponement of the exams. The Twitter hashtag #ProtestAgainstExamsinCovid garnered over three million

tweets in a single day. The student community also held relay
hunger strikes in protest.

In the blink of an eye, politicians jumped into the fray,
as they are expected to do. Leaders from various political
parties—like the Congress, Aam Aadmi Party, Trinamool
Congress and Rashtriya Janata Dal—expressed reservations
about conducting such career-determining exams in the
midst of a pandemic and urged the Centre to come up with
an alternative solution for admissions into medical and
engineering courses.

I, too, joined the chorus of voices that wanted the
government to do a serious rethink on it. I tweeted in support
of the troubled students, calling for the postponement of the
NEET and JEE-Main 2020 exams.

On 26 August, I tweeted: 'This is not an examination
only for students. It's an examination for the Government
too. Govt. has an opportunity to excel by postponing #JEE_
NEET for 60 days. Make it happen and bring those smiles
back. Students & Govt. can prepare in this time window.
#PostponeJEE_NEET.'

I added (in Hindi), 'Tomorrow will be built on the
strength of the younger generation. It is our responsibility
to carry forward their enthusiasm sensibly, to put on
positive forces.'

I strongly felt that there was nothing wrong with the
youth trying to reach out to the government and believed
that a dialogue-based decision should be made in the interest
of the students. On the other hand, the loss of an academic
year was of equal concern. Academicians said that a further
delay in examinations would disrupt the academic calendar

and put the future of students in jeopardy. They further emphasized that conducting the exams in September would allow institutes to start online classes at the very least. The Supreme Court also observed, 'Life must go on' and students 'cannot waste a whole year'.

A sizeable percentage of the student population in India was crestfallen when the Supreme Court ruled that the JEE-Main and NEET exams could not be deferred. Six ministers of Opposition-ruled states had approached the SC against its order, which allowed the exams to be held despite the increase in COVID-19 cases in the country. On 4 September, the SC rejected their petitions. In any case, some batches of JEE had already been held by then.

The government did what it could in these trying circumstances. The NTA claimed that appropriate arrangements had been made to conduct the entrance examinations, with utmost regard for safety measures. The agency also said that over 99 per cent of the candidates had been assigned their 'first choice of centre cities'.

In order to ensure that social distancing was maintained, the NTA said it had increased the number of centres for 2020. While the number of centres for the JEE was hiked from 570 to 660, those for the NEET went from 2546 to 3843. As per the standard operating procedure developed by the NTA, fewer candidates would be seated in exam rooms to maintain social distancing. (In the case of NEET, the number of candidates per room was reduced from twenty-four to twelve.) Students were asked to use gloves and masks at all times, and centres were instructed to be equipped with extra supplies in case students or staff needed it.

Hand sanitizers would be installed at entry and exit points. Students would be dispersed in a staggered manner to avoid overcrowding. Thermo guns would be used to check the body temperature of all staff and candidates. If any examination functionary failed to meet the self-declaration criteria or pass the thermal-scanner check, they would be asked to leave the examination centre immediately.

The NTA promised, 'No one will be denied permission to appear for the examination, if he/she violates the Covid-19 directives/advisories of Government (Central/State) applicable on the day of exam and instructions mentioned in the Admit Card.' To implement this, isolation rooms were to be set up for students whose body temperature was over 99.4 degrees Fahrenheit.

Ideally, these exams should have been postponed. But I respected the order of the Supreme Court. Since the exams could not be pushed, I decided to do the next best thing. I made up my mind to help the students who lived in distant places reach their exam centres.

To quote a newspaper report, 'Everyone is aware of how actor Sonu Sood has extended his help and support to each and every layman during the pandemic crisis. From arranging buses for migrants to buying flight tickets for needy to reach home, Sonu Sood has stood like a solid rock. Now, the actor has extended help to students who will appear for Joint Entrance Examinations (JEE) and National Eligibility Entrance Test (NEET), scheduled to be held in September.'

Taking to Twitter, I made an open, unconditional offer on 28 August and said, 'Incase #JEE_NEET happens: To all the students who will be appearing & are struck in flood hit areas

One-year-old me.

Post my mundan ceremony in Moga, Punjab, when they shaved my head. My mom took me to a local photo studio to get this clicked. I still have the sari she is wearing.

On the same day, after my mundan ceremony. This picture is very special to me.

At a studio in Moga.

With Mona, my elder sister.
I am three years old here, and
my sister four and a half.

Malvika (my younger sister),
Dad, Mona and me at our
house in Moga.

Malvika, my dad and me. We were celebrating Malvika's birthday in Moga.

My best friend, Sanjiv, and I won the first prize when we partnered in a sack race at Sacred Heart School, Moga.

Mom feeding me cake during my ninth birthday celebrations at our home in Moga.

With my sister Mona,
at our home in Moga.

With Malvika, at our
home in Moga.

Celebrating Rakhi with
my sisters, Mona and
Malvika.

In Moga, when we had organized a small gathering on the festival of Lohri.

Sonali and me, at our wedding on 28 December 2000.

When Malvika visited me on the sets of *Happy New Year*.

With my sisters. When
we visited Mona in
Maryland, USA.

In Bangkok,
with Malvika.

In Bangkok, on a family trip.
This picture has Sonali, Gautam,
Gunnu, Eshaan, Ayaan and me.

On a holiday in Bangkok, two years ago. With Malvika, Gautam and my niece, Nyra.

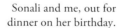

Sonali and me, out for dinner on her birthday.

With my niece Anushka, my brother-in-law Rajesh Sharma and Sonali in the US.

On a holiday in London, with
Sonali, Eshaan and Ayaan.

With my mom. We had this picture
taken at a photo studio in Mumbai
because Mom had pointed out that we
had few pictures together. Today, I wish
I could create new memories with her.

The Sood family.

of Bihar, Assam & Gujrat. Do let me know ur areas of travel. Trying to make ur travel arrangements to reach ur examination centres. No one should miss their exam bec of resources.'

This was a unique situation, a one-off, pandemic-related problem faced by students appearing for entrance exams. However, my mind swung to a more long-term help that I could offer to students.

'Behind all your stories is always your mother's story, because hers is where yours begins,' said author, philanthropist and musician Mitch Albom. My mother's story was inextricably twined with mine.

Once the predicament of students was registered on my radar, I activated my charity organization, Sood Charity Foundation, and through it was introduced the Professor Saroj Sood Scholarship. What better tribute could I pay to my mother than this? My mother's biggest love was education. And the education of underprivileged students was the burning passion of her life. She lived to educate people and was consumed by this cause until her dying day. She wanted me, too, to keep the education torch burning in my lifetime. A scholarship in her name was the most fitting epitaph I could inscribe in her memory.

Among the many cases I have encountered of families facing difficulties and trying to overcome them during the lockdown, one recurring theme has been of dwindling income to educate children. Stories abound of parents who are willing but are unable to come up with the required fees for their children's education.

Five hundred is but a drop in the vast ocean of students. But I had to make a beginning somewhere, and I have begun with 500. Small but significant, because it is a partial fulfilment of my mother's big dream. Each year, my charity organization will award the Prof. Saroj Sood Scholarship to 500 students from various fields like medicine, engineering and business management. We'll take care of all their fees, right from admission time to their graduation. I have partnered with a host of universities in different parts of India, and we'll offer this scholarship to students whose parents can't fund their education.

Quoting me, the *Times of India*, on 12 September, said, 'During the past few months, I have seen how the underprivileged struggle to pay for their children's education. While some did not have phones to attend online classes, others did not have money to pay the fees. So, I have tied up with various universities across the country to offer scholarships under the name of my mother, Professor Saroj Sood.'

For me, this has been a watershed year which rerouted my entire life. On 13 October 2020, my mother's thirteenth death anniversary, I honoured her memory in a way that hadn't struck the old (or earlier) me. With thorough research on 'just-what-we-should-do-for-society-now', attuned to the many slots of emptiness that exist in society, I announced a monetary fund for 250–300 brainy IAS aspirants. Our country needs the best-trained minds to take it forward with their administrative adroitness. But the Indian Administrative Service exams are so tough to crack that channelized coaching is essential even for the brilliant. This is where I knew I could be of assistance by providing aid to the brightest students who need that extra coaching to become IAS officers. It seemed so apt to float this fund on my mother's death anniversary.

'Biology is the least of what makes someone a mother.' You said it, Oprah Winfrey. Professor Saroj Sood was more than a biological bond for me. What she stood for in her life went far beyond blood ties. Her passion for education has become an indelible part of my own life. So, this one's for you, Mom.

2

A Signature Becomes an Autograph

Naaku chaala truptiga vundi.

That's Telugu for 'I'm feeling a sense of contentment'.

It's the language I returned to once the lockdown was lifted and the acting community resumed work after a gap of seven long months. For most of the world, it was about picking up the threads once again and going back to where they'd left things off in mid-March. But for me, a new Sonu Sood had fluttered out of the cocoon of the pandemic. It wasn't only about the soul-gratifying transformation I'd undergone as a human being. When I stepped back into the world, it was as if everyone was looking at me with new eyes.

Naaku yentho santhosamga vundi. I'm feeling rather elated; rather happy.

I returned to the studios in Hyderabad with the Telugu film *Kandireega 2*, sequel to the commercially well-received romantic action comedy of 2011. *Kandireega* (which translates to 'wasp') starred Ram, Hansika Motwani and me, and it was remade in Hindi as *Main Tera Hero*, with Varun Dhawan, Ileana D'Cruz and Nargis Fakhri in 2014. Nine years had elapsed since the original was released.

When I went back to work in October 2020, it felt like I was stepping into a completely new order. It began with the flight itself. There was an unfamiliar anticipation, like one was catching a plane for the first time in one's life. To go through the checklist of dos and don'ts, with SOPs in place at the airport and on the flight, was anxiety-inducing. I was going to face the camera after a break of 200-odd days, and it already felt strange, as if I hadn't put in twenty-plus years of non-stop work.

I was grateful that my wife, Sonali, accompanied me to Hyderabad on this trip. Her presence comforted me. She threw an invisible duvet of security around me. She watched over me while I made it my life's mission to look out for others.

But the new bag of feelings I took off with was a minor change as compared to what awaited me at the studio. I was looking forward to sniffing the studio air, the aroma of filter coffee and being in the company of colleagues once again. Such a great feeling! But the real change became evident the moment I reached the studio, took a step out of the car and was accorded . . . a hero's welcome.

It was only then that it dawned on me that this was no ordinary day at work. The entire unit was actually awaiting my arrival. In true south Indian style, I was greeted with a shawl, a mark of respect, and given bouquets of flowers, with good wishes showered on me like confetti. The euphoria was like shots of caffeine. My dear colleague and co-star Prakash Raj unstintingly applauded and told me how proud he was of me.

It felt so right to begin my new post-COVID innings in the south. I have a special connect with the people there, perhaps because my star trek began in the south. I have been perpetually rewarded with an abundance of love and respect in these states. But this tidal wave of adulation was incredible. It had little to do with my success as a star and was singularly caused by what had unfolded during the pandemic.

'Go not to the temple to pray on bended knees. First bend down to lift someone who is downtrodden.' I bow before the sagacity of Nobel laureate Rabindranath Tagore. Affability can attract affection; success in the work sphere can draw applause; but it's utter selflessness and single-minded service to humanity that get you the love and respect of people. That trip to Hyderabad inspired me, more than ever, to escalate my efforts to keep working towards the betterment of society.

That my new-found 'superman' image had percolated into my career became a reality for me when director Santosh had to actually sit down and rework my character in *Kandireega 2*. In the pre-lockdown script my role had shades of grey. But in the ensuing seven months, when I switched lanes in my personal life, my humanitarian work would no longer allow even fictional villainy to taint my name. For one scene, Prakash Raj had to angrily hold me by my collar. Yet, despite all of us knowing that we were in a make-believe world, he flatly refused to do so, saying that the Sonu he now knew couldn't be treated in such an uncouth manner.

He reasoned that with the kind of reputation I currently enjoyed, I could no longer be roughed up on screen.

Prakash Raj wasn't the only one who felt that my image had become indubitably larger than life. It's odd to flog this sentiment but with my public image mutating so phenomenally, everybody agreed that giving me negative roles would no longer be publicly acceptable. They had to do a serious rethink on my entire character, and all the scenes that featured me called for an overhaul of the screenplay. We therefore ended up having to reschedule a twenty-day shoot.

Holding forth and airing opinions is no way to change perceptions. It's only setting an example with actual action that can bring about change. I saw this change when everyone in the studio—from the toilet attendants to the catering staff—greeted me with the warmest of smiles and a respectful namaste. They had done it earlier too. But now, one could perceive the light of hope that shone in their eyes when they saw me.

A pitiful situation unfolded in that very studio one day. A six-year-old boy, named Harshwardhan Deshaboina, with chronic end-stage liver disease, walked in with his parents, Lakshmi and Nagaraju. He required immediate medical attention, and his father, who was a conductor with the Telangana State Road Transport Corporation, could ill afford the expense of getting Harshwardhan operated.

When the parents approached me at the studio, appealing that I help save their child, none of us could hold back tears. The plight of the child, his stomach protruding and his skin sallow, melted every heart on the premises. I was so moved that I had to take action without delay. The operation little

Harshwardhan needed urgently was expensive, and I had to involve quite a few people to gather the requisite funds.

But with the guidance of the Almighty, we did it. In mid-October, Harshwardhan was wheeled into the OT and the operation was performed. He's currently recuperating.

The idea behind narrating the story of Harshwardhan—whose name figures on the long list of patients we have assisted with life-saving surgeries over the past few months—is solely to put under the spotlight the pressing need for awareness. When it comes to health care for the needy, we are staring into a vast and bottomless pit of misery. There is so much more that needs to be done; there are so many children congenitally afflicted, with poverty compounding their distress, that this world needs not a handful but a legion of Sonu Soods.

'One person can make a difference. And everyone should try,' said John F. Kennedy. Become a person who saves lives, who brings joy where sorrow lives and light where darkness prevails. It's no coincidence that I met the migrants on the highway; it was God's plan. That crucial first step which can change the direction in which your life is heading, take it. Make that beginning—it's never too small. As artist Andy Warhol urged, 'They always say time changes things, but you actually have to change them yourself.'

So don't wait. There's never a perfect time. But there's always a perfect beginning, and that is now.

Naaku chaala baaga anipisthunnadi.

I feel good. Good to be the medium that brought timely help to Harshwardhan, and I hope to be one for others like him.

It's a multiplication of the dopamine effect that service to humanity brings into your life. You don't seek applause; that's never the end goal. But when you're cheered from the sidelines for the social work you do, it fills your heart with joy.

After that celebratory comeback to the studios, an encore awaited me in Mumbai. On set at Yashraj Studios, when I started shooting with Akshay Kumar for *Prithviraj* after a long spell of 210-plus days, my entry sparked off a round of applause. But I knew that the ovation was not for Sonu Sood; it was for the work that I have become committed to.

It's been a life rich with such rewards, far more priceless than trophies on the shelf. These rewards motivate me to soldier on. You know it's the right path when you feel good about treading further and further and never want to turn back.

Just two more words: Join me.

3

A Tractor in Time Saves a Farmer

Name: Nageswara Rao (and family)
Location: Chittoor, Andhra Pradesh
Problem: Manual ploughing of the farms by daughters, necessitated by pandemic-induced poverty
The way out: A tractor for the family and education for the daughters

Dedicated to those who work in acres, not hours. These are not my own lines; I recall having read them once. Borrowed lines but such a perfect fit when I flip the pages of my memory and think of the visual that arrested me on that Saturday, 25 July 2020.

A journalist, Krishnamurthy—to whom I'm indebted for bringing this to my awareness—had uploaded a video clip and tweeted about a tomato farmer in Madanapalle in Chittoor district. The farmer's daughters were being used, instead of the traditional oxen, to plough his field.

It was so disturbing; not an image you wanted to see. Those girls should have been in school and not pulling the plough. Yet another picture of despair thrown up by the pandemic. However, I wasn't willing to let it get me down.

That visual was stuck in my head—a poverty-stricken father giving a hand to his daughters while the mother scattered fertilizer on the fields. When I'm troubled, I have internal debates with myself. That day, I told myself that on the one hand we claim our daughters are our pride, while on the other we let our daughters plough the field like oxen.

'Vision without action remains a dream,' said author and executive Joel Barker. I couldn't just sit back and imagine that my empathy from miles away would telepathically alter the destiny of the two young girls. I had to be the man of action that I knew myself to be.

Once again, my many years of work in Andhra Pradesh stood me in good stead as I tapped my contacts in the state to find out more about this farmer and his family. Within hours, the details poured in. I learnt that his name was Nageswara Rao, and the distressing visual on social media was from his farm in a village close to Chittoor. Although I've shot extensively in the state, I'd never been to Chittoor district. Now, this became one more place on my list of must-visit places.

By 9.30 p.m. that same Saturday, my friends from Andhra provided me with further details. They even gave me his phone number, and I connected with Nageswara Rao personally. He told me that he ran a tea stall in Madanapalle, his village. But the pandemic had forced the shutters down on his small business, making him stare at penury and hunger.

My people in Andhra had already ferreted out details of how pitiable his and his family's condition was.

On the spur of the moment, I promised Nageswara that I would immediately arrange two oxen for him, so that his girls could be taken off the yoke. He was so excited at my offer that he called me back within minutes to say that the oxen were available in Tirupati, and once he had the money, he could rush there and buy them.

Without giving it much thought, I assured Nageswara that he'd get the money to buy the oxen. It took a few more moments for the tube light in my brain to light up as I realized that a tractor—and not oxen—would be the ideal solution to this family's problems. If animals were employed on the field, more than one person would still be needed to toil along with the oxen, while a tractor would ease their lives considerably. So, I changed my mind and informed Nageswara that instead of sending him money for oxen, I'd have a tractor delivered to him the very next day. But I needed a promise from him in return—that he would see to it that his daughters pursued their education.

The hearty Punjabi in me had spoken on an impulse. But shortly after that conversation, reality hit me. I twisted and turned in my sleep. The next day was a Sunday and we were under a lockdown. How on earth was I going to keep my promise to Nageswara and have a tractor on his field the next day? But I'd given my word. *Punjabiyaan da vaada* mattered.

Here I must tell you that Punjabis are passionate about farming. We empathize with the farming community in more ways than one. Another aside is, a tractor is something every young boy from Punjab has either driven or ridden on.

Fortunately for me, by now my reputation preceded me. People everywhere wanted to help in whatever way they could and be a part of this social movement. On Sunday morning, I called my friend Karan Gilhotra, who is from Chandigarh, and asked him to find out the contact of an agency in Andhra Pradesh, because I wanted a tractor delivered to a farmer on an SOS basis. I stressed to him that I needed that tractor to be delivered to Nageswara that very day. Karan called up the local Andhra agent of Sonalika Tractors, one of the leading tractor companies in India. Though it was their weekly off, when the guys realized that the request had come from me and was really important, they expedited my request. And voila!—around 5 p.m. the same day, Nageswara had a brand-new tractor standing on his field.

The next thing I knew was that the farmer and his family were on the phone line to me, all teary but thrilled. They were moved and excited with the unexpected gift that had landed in their lives. In fact, it was like a joyous celebration for the entire village as the arrival of the tractor became the event of the season. Realizing how important the farming vehicle was to all of them, I asked Nageswara to promise me that he would allow others in the village to also use the tractor from time to time. He was only too happy to agree to that.

They say that when you do an act of kindness, the left hand shouldn't know what the right hand is doing. But Ghar Bhejo and what it has burgeoned into is not the sort of movement where one has to be publicity-shy. On the contrary, it pays to let the world know what you're doing, for it is invigorating to see how many people are inspired by it and are willing to pitch in.

My conversations with Nageswara Rao, which were all available on social media, attracted the attention of N. Chandrababu Naidu, former chief minister of undivided Andhra Pradesh. I was a huge fan of his when I did a spate of Telugu films in Hyderabad. Looking at the progress the state had made under him, I had once remarked that I wished every state in India had a CM like him. So it was a special honour when Chandrababu-garu noticed my interest in Nageswara Rao's welfare and joined the social bandwagon. Mr Naidu spoke to me on Sunday night and said, 'Sonu-garu, what you have done for Andhra, I can't express in words.'

Naidu Sir also added, 'Sonu, we politicians and local actors must learn from you how to action things. What you have done for Andhra Pradesh at a sensitive time like the pandemic is simply amazing.' He followed up the phone call by tweeting that he was impressed by my 'inspiring effort' and promised that he in turn would take care of the education of the farmer's daughters. He said he would get the state to look after the girls.

I share his exact words: 'Spoke with @SonuSood ji & applauded him for his inspiring effort to send a tractor to Nageswara Rao's family in Chittoor District. Moved by the plight of the family, I have decided to take care of the education of the two daughters and help them pursue their dreams.'

I promptly tweeted my gratitude to him: 'Thank you so much sir for all the encouraging words. Your kindness will inspire everyone to come forward and help the needy. Under your guidance millions will find a way to achieve their dreams. Keep inspiring sir. I look forward to meeting you soon.'

'One person can make a difference. And everyone should try.' Yes, John F. Kennedy, I agree.

The tractor tale is an episode that keeps whirring in my mind. They say a picture speaks a thousand words. It does, for it was that single image of those girls on the field with their parents behind them that got frozen in my mind and got me to act.

It's all about the right timing too. Had I missed that tweet or that image, life may not have undergone the change it did for this family in Andhra Pradesh.

All the rescue operations and timely interventions that my team and I have made over the last four months have also made me philosophical. There can be nothing good about a global pandemic that claims lives and throws the world economy into miserable disarray. Yet it was the life-threatening COVID-19 menace that brought me face to face with the deplorable levels of poverty our people live in. And it changed my life forever. Today, when you sit down at the dinner table, you can't help but give a thought to how little most people subsist on.

Every case that comes up before me is filled with pathos untold. A widowed lady in Telangana, who lost her husband one year ago, was bringing up three young children on her own. She was bravely battling the odds, feeding and raising her three children—one boy, named Manohar, and two girls—when the pandemic struck. She succumbed to it, leaving her three kids orphaned and at the mercy of the villagers who were initially willing to take care of them. But they, too, were bearing the brunt of the pandemic, which made it impossible for them to feed three more mouths on a regular basis.

That was when someone from there tagged me on Twitter, asking me to help these kids.

My team sprang to action and flew the kids from Telangana to Shirdi. We have put all three of them in an institution in Shirdi, where they will be cared for and will also receive their school education. Manohar is spirited and has shown a willingness to study hard and become a doctor. He's also got ambitions for his sisters and would like one of them to join the police force. I know it's way too early to predict their future, but at least the capacity for dreaming is intact in these little children. For the moment, it gives me peace of mind to know that we have been able to nestle this displaced family in a safe institution in Shirdi and ensure their welfare and education.

It's been coming from all directions, all states. A rickshaw-puller in Punjab lost his life due to spurious liquor, along with 125 others. It was tragic because he couldn't get medical help on time. Worse was to befall his family when his lifeless body sent his wife into a shock, and she too died on the spot. This was similar to the Telangana case, as the parents' deaths had left three young kids orphaned here too. They were aged nine, six and three, too young to even know what had hit them. Once again, the villagers couldn't take on the responsibility of bringing up the three children.

My team and I organized a home for them and made sure that they were enrolled in schools. We also set aside funds for the upkeep of these kids, and we have been keeping a close eye on them, constantly monitoring their progress.

We got to know about these six kids from Telangana and Punjab and could step into their lives. But what about the thousands more out there who haven't been able to reach us or anybody else? We need so many more people to open their hearts and help the distressed.

'Chaos in the world brings uneasiness, but it also allows the opportunity for creativity and growth,' said the US politician Tom Barrett. I'd tweak it to say chaos and uneasiness gives us an opportunity to change and expand the heart.

There is a Chinese proverb that says, 'The best time to plant a tree was twenty years ago. The second-best time is now.' I've planted mine.

The Andhra Relationship Further Cemented

Andhra Pradesh and I have developed a special bond that I continue to nurture in various ways. The same journalist who'd uploaded that video about the Chittoor farmer, Krishnamurthy, later tweeted, 'Inspired by @Sonu Sood(not kidding!) 2 villages in #Vizianagaram dt of # Andhra Pradesh decided to stand on their own feet. After begging the local govt since 1947 to build a road to access the village on a hill top, each family pooled in Rs.2000 to build a road themselves!'

Krishnamurthy added how the only mode of transport for around 250 families in the Chintamala and Kodama villages of Salur Mandal was the *doli*, or palanquin. Pregnant women had to depend on this for emergencies. Overall, Rs 20 lakh was collected, courtesy the two loans and the contribution of Rs 2000 from each family. The villagers then hired JCBs from neighbouring Odisha to build the 4 km ghat road. This whole thing was testified to by Kalisetti Appala

Naidu, president, Public Awareness Forum, who has been coordinating with the villagers.

I have always believed that in life one must try to build a bridge, not a wall. This is an important life lesson for all. Whether it is in our homes, society or in public life, bridges help cement relationships. Walls separate. We must choose responsibly.

4

Uplifted by Airlift

Name: Too many to list; 177 in all
Description: Workers
Place to be evacuated from: Kochi, Kerala
Destination: Bhubaneswar, Odisha
Reason: Stranded without work or shelter

I have worked in a variety of films and played a wide range of characters. But I have stayed largely unaffected by the make-believe world that I immerse myself in during working hours. Barring maybe a few roles, which I carried home and which I can literally count on my fingers. Because those characters seeped into my system. For example, freedom fighter Bhagat Singh in *Shaheed-e-Azam* (2002), or for that matter, Pasupati from my film *Arundhati* (2009), the character for which I won the prestigious Nandi Award. Except for these projects, what happened before the camera or on screen didn't really resonate with my personal life. I certainly never experienced the feeling that something had jumped out of celluloid to become a flesh-and-blood moment for me. But that too changed after the pandemic. I was in the midst of sending waves of people home when I went through another gooseflesh-raising episode.

A movie in which I had no part to play but which nonetheless affected me deeply was the inspirational *Airlift* (2016), directed by Raja Krishna Menon. In this film, Akshay Kumar played a Kuwait-based Indian businessman named Ranjit Katyal. I had my heart in my mouth when the protagonist evacuated 1,70,000 Indians from Kuwait after Saddam Hussein attacked the country; and I felt a lump in my throat when Akshay raised the Indian tricolour at the end of a victorious airlift. Patriotic films usually have that effect on me. And for some reason, *Airlift*, the movie, stayed with me; it had that kind of strong impact on me.

The inexplicable connection I had with this film showed up on 29 May 2020. I felt a sense of déjà vu when, in the midst of the lockdown, I managed to evacuate and airlift a large group of people from one state to another. A total of 177 men and women had to be picked up from Kochi, Kerala, and carried to safety in Bhubaneswar, Odisha. There was so much detailing in the plan and such fine points to be covered in the execution that I felt I was watching *Airlift* again.

My personal *Airlift* thriller, as true to life as Akshay's film, began with a message on my Twitter timeline. I was informed that there were 167 women stranded in Ernakulam close to Kochi, Kerala, who needed to be rescued and sent to Odisha. They worked in an embroidery workshop. There were ten boys too, who were plumbers, electricians and miscellaneous job workers in and around the factory premises.

The factory had closed soon after the lockdown was imposed in Kerala, leaving these Odia workers high and dry. The women had no shelter and hardly any food in Kerala. They also barely knew Malayalam, the state's language. In short, they were cash-strapped and helpless. But help comes from the most unexpected sources. Someone guided these women to reach out to me, and that's when I got their message on my Twitter timeline.

It was a massive, mind-numbing operation for my team and me. There was no local transport available to fetch this group of women from the factory premises where they were bunched up. They had but one intense desire: 'Come what may, we want to go home.' I learnt that they all hailed from the same district, Kendrapara, in Odisha.

With local transport unavailable and airports all over the country closed, we had to obtain permissions and coordinate at several levels. Once again, an engineer's blueprint for action had to be drawn.

Accordingly, I first reached out to some authorities at Air Asia. Once they were convinced about the immediacy and the integrity of my request, they agreed to send an aircraft from Bengaluru to Kochi to airlift the girls and take them to Bhubaneswar. In Kerala, we had to arrange for a minimum of seven large buses to fetch the 167 women from Ernakulam and drop them off at the Kochi airport in time to catch the flight. But it was not smooth sailing.

When the buses were loaded, there was a crisis. The ten men, the assorted plumbers and other workers who had also been stranded in and around the factory, wanted to join the women and go home. However, the security guards at the factory did not allow them to board the bus. When one of them dialled me and pleaded for help, another round of talks ensued, this time with the security personnel at the factory. They were convinced and permitted the men to board the buses. As in every operation, whether it was by bus, train or plane, I had to be available round the clock to pick up the phone to sort out last-minute glitches and seek eleventh-hour clearances. It wasn't possible to delegate responsibility and go lock myself up in an air-conditioned bedroom. It was my voice that opened doors; I had to be on call.

I cannot count the number of phone calls that went back and forth to meet the challenge of opening up two airports, Kochi and Bhubaneswar. Until the airport authorities in both cities were convinced that it was an emergency operation, that this group of men and women had to get back home, I had to keep speaking to people. I could breathe only when both airports were opened for this flight to take off and land.

The journey of the factory workers began at 3 a.m. They flew out of Kochi at around 5 in the morning and landed in Bhubaneswar at around 10.30 a.m. Initially, until they were well on their way, there was much trepidation among the 177 evacuees; they wondered what lay ahead of them. In Mumbai, we were going through our own nail-biting moments. There was anxiety at every turn for us. We were fully aware that one slip-up anywhere and the whole operation would be botched.

For close to twenty hours, I went sleepless. Until the Air Asia plane touched down at Bhubaneswar, I was on tenterhooks. It was only after they reached their homes in Kendrapara that I could allow my eyelids to droop.

After my own Mission Airlift, I could fully understand the strain and scale of the operation and the satisfaction that businessman Ranjit Katyal must have felt when he brought his countrymen, who'd been stranded in Kuwait, safely back to India. This was a rare full circle of life imitating art, which had imitated life. My real-life airlift felt like the Akshay Kumar movie, which in turn had been inspired by a true story.

For those 177 people, it was understandably a twin ecstasy. I had set out to usher them home to safety, as I had done with the migrants who were sent home by buses and trains. But for the Kerala to Odisha passengers, it was almost like an odyssey, as their trauma turned to thrill. For most of them, a ride on a plane was a first-time experience, one they cherished and would narrate breathlessly to their families. So, unwittingly, I had provided a treat for them and not just a passage back home.

I believe that it's not happy hearts that burst with thankfulness; it's thankful hearts that burst with happiness. My Odia friends showed their gratitude in many ways. The day they reached home, they showered me with text messages, and for the next two months, many of them touched base with me regularly. I'd get a message every morning, and they'd go to sleep only after sending a goodnight wish. Gratitude overflowed in some of them as they made emotional vows like, 'Sonu Bhai, we can give our lives for you.' It was all very touching, because it was not lip service; it came from deep within.

One of the 177 passengers, who was grateful to have been sent home by plane, got a life-size cut-out of mine made and put it up at a square in Bhubaneswar and garlanded it along with the others.

What do you do when you wake up in the morning and find yourself in a cartoon that's captioned 'Where there is hope, there is Sonu Sood'? It came with a picture of mine: 'Humanity' was written across my neck, 'Vaccine' across my torso, and 'Till vaccine comes our only saviour' was the caption. My sole reaction on Twitter was to send two emojis—folded hands of thankfulness and a blushing face.

Because that's how I truly feel. I feel a surge of gratitude at the overwhelming, encouraging applause which acts as a booster to keep me going in the same direction. Simultaneously, I feel humble and shy when I see all those 'superman' labels. I am but a man, fortunate to have been handpicked to lead such a movement.

An actor meets all kinds of admirers; you see a lot of hero worship. But this kind of adulation is totally different from the idolization of a matinee star that happens from an immeasurable distance. You know that when a migrant opens his shop in your name or names her baby after you, the feeling is different. It was validation that I'd done something right. This validation moved me to do more.

And opportunity came tapping on my window once again. Like those who'd got home by bus and train and had come in droves, when information about the Kochi–Bhubaneswar flight took wing and reached faraway Kyrgyzstan, it was another learning experience for me. From two states, it became two countries and two continents where one had to liaise with and convince authorities. Visuals of students holding up my poster inside the plane that evacuated them from Kyrgyzstan surfaced all over.

You can't plan this. It's been amazing. I've never been to Kyrgyzstan, but today I feel a deep connection with it. I want to see the country. I want to go to Kendrapara and see the welding shop. I want to go to Darbhanga and see that little infant. From a Moga boy I've grown into a global man.

After I'd successfully arranged air transport for 4000 stranded students from Kyrgyzstan to India, requests for a passage to India came to me from Canada, Uzbekistan and the Philippines. Honestly, every person who reaches out to me and places such faith in me energizes me.

'A man of courage is also full of faith,' said the Roman statesman Cicero. I am blessed with the courage to dive in, and I have faith that I will reach the shore.

I'm one of the welders who Sonu Sood Sir airlifted from Kerala to Kendrapara. I have my aged parents, my wife and two daughters, all of whom were anxious about my return home. Now it has been months since my return, and I have opened my own welding shop, which I have named after Sonu Sood Sir. Business is very slow because things around our village have taken a beating in the pandemic. But I will hang in there. It almost feels like a second innings, because what stared at us at the peak of the pandemic seemed like a dark fate. How do we express our gratitude to Sonu Sir? I guess, we have to work hard and stay motivated.'

—Prashant Kumar Pradhan

5

Tragedy Strikes Three

Names: Simhati Sudhir, Santosh Mani and Aman Kathed
Date: June 2020
Source: Melbourne, Sydney and Darwin in Australia
Destination: Odisha, Madhya Pradesh
Reason: Father's death

'Coincidence doesn't happen a third time.'

Whoever spouted this piece of wisdom as a quotable quote should have been with our movement during the lockdown. It was incredibly eerie, but the terrible similarity in the three unrelated cases amounted to a tragic coincidence.

I got three SOS calls, from three different parts of Australia, with one common thread: all three boys on the other side of the phone wanted to come home to India to perform the last rites of their respective fathers. Stuck in a faraway continent when tragedy struck their families, three boys with different backgrounds couldn't reach their hometowns because of restricted air traffic and quarantine restrictions on arrival in India.

I could completely empathize with all three of them, because three years after the loss of my father, I have still to come to terms with it. I understand how special the father–son relationship is. 'To lose your father is to lose the one whose guidance and help you seek, who supports you like a tree trunk supports its branches.' Canadian author and Man Booker Prize winner Yann Martel, of *Life of Pi* fame, got it right. Losing a father is like a tree losing its trunk; we are but one of its branches.

As I have mentioned earlier, I lost my father with the suddenness of an unexpected thunderbolt on 7 February 2016, and to this day the sadness engulfs me.

Yet, unlike those three boys from Australia—who were miles away but whose loss struck an emotional chord with me—I was fortunate to have been with my father in Moga on his last day. I cannot express how much it meant to me that I had spent the entire day with him, little knowing that when we retired to our rooms after saying goodnight, it was actually farewell forever. I went to bed a happy man, because I had got a whole day with my father and didn't have even an inkling that I would not see him alive ever again.

But that was how it played out. Life dealt me a really cruel blow when, at the midnight hour, he had a heart attack, and before my younger sister and I could rush him to hospital, he'd taken his last breath. My grief was unfathomable. I still think of it as a nightmare from which I will wake up one day and find my father next to me.

In an address to high school graduates, Michelle Obama once said about the loss of her father, 'Let me tell you, he is the hole in my heart. His loss is my scar.' I could sense the hole in the heart of those three boys who called me for help, so they could return home from Australia and attend their fathers' funerals. I knew exactly the bewildered emptiness that they were feeling. It stirred me and made me want to personally speak to each of them. I wanted to provide the balm, however temporary, for their emotional pain.

Simhati Sudhir was in Melbourne when his father passed away in Odisha, and he wanted to be home to perform the last rites and be with his family at such a tragic time. Santosh Mani was a student in Sydney and had to travel to Bhubaneswar via Delhi for the same reasons as Simhati. The two didn't even know each other, but their circumstances were uncannily similar. Sharing the same kind of grief was twenty-five-year-old Aman Kathed; he worked in Darwin and wanted to reach Nagda in Madhya Pradesh.

Someone once said, 'Coincidence is God's way of remaining anonymous.' There was a God above who had guided these boys to me.

Sometime in mid-June, a boy called Rakesh reached out to my Ghar Bhejo colleague and close associate Neeti Goel on Instagram. He told her that his friend Aman had lost his father and needed to travel to India. Once she had the details, Neeti briefed me about the death of Pradeep Kathed in MP and his son's predicament in Australia. It immediately made me set the machinery we had in place going, use all the influence and see to it that young Aman was on a flight from Sydney to Delhi.

I spoke to Suman Singh, an IAS officer in Delhi, who helped Aman get out of the airport as soon as he landed and drive to Nagda. His father was only in his fifties and was hale and hearty when he suffered a cardiac arrest. Aman had a stunned, grief-stricken mother and a younger brother waiting for him at home. Both of them needed Aman for moral support.

I spoke to Aman several times to ensure that he'd been given everything he needed for a quick return to India and to also check if he could hold himself emotionally together at such a vulnerable moment. I was very impressed with his demeanour. Aman is the resident engagement officer at Charles Darwin University and is in charge of the welfare of international students enrolled there for graduation and post-graduation studies. Perhaps because of his job profile, he seemed mature, sorted and capable. Although shaken by his father's unanticipated demise, he didn't go to pieces and controlled himself splendidly.

As Diana Der Hovanessian, the Armenian–American poet, wrote in her poem 'Shifting in the Sun', 'When your father dies, say the Armenians, your sun shifts forever, and you walk in his light.' Like me, I'm sure the boys will find a path, lit by their fathers, to walk on.

I could identify with the three boys because I understand the sentiments that bind us to our families so deeply. The loss of a parent is irreparable. I could also comprehend that they had to rush to their respective hometowns to attend a ritual for such a heart-rending tragedy.

In those days, passengers arriving from anywhere were required to be in quarantine for fourteen days. So when the boys landed in New Delhi, they, too, had to adhere to Government of India regulations. But circumstances called upon the boys to leave the airport without any delay. I intervened on their behalf, spoke to the health authorities at the airport and impressed upon them how imperative it was for the three boys to directly reach their homes to pay their last respects. I made a personal and special request that they allow the boys to go home from the airport. But I also told the boys that they must self-quarantine at home immediately after the ceremony.

Long after his father's funeral, Aman spoke to me at length. In fact, we had many conversations till the time he flew back to his university in September. Before he left, he called me to convey the deep gratitude he felt towards Neeti, Suman Singh and me for our compassion and timely support. He told me, 'Sonu Sir, what I have taken away from this experience is that you do not need to know a person to help him. Succour can sometimes come from a complete stranger. I was a stranger for you and yet you helped me more than a relative or a friend would have. I have learnt from this and will always remember it. Like you, I too will make sure that I'm useful to strangers all through my life. I will go out of my way to help people because I have personally seen how you stood there like a rock and saw me through my moment of despair.'

The German aviator and religious leader Dieter F. Uchtdorf preached, 'As we lose ourselves in the service of others, we discover our own lives and our own happiness.' I've been on this joyous journey of self-discovery since April 2020. Going by Aman's promise, I have, hopefully, set off a positive chain reaction.

6

Health Is Wealth: A Cure for Many Ills

It's not pieces of silver but health that's real wealth. Going by that aphorism, perhaps the poverty line should be measured by who has easy access to health care. The doorway to health care should not depend on where you live or how much money you have in your pocket.

Way back in 1966, Dr Martin Luther King Jr said, 'Of all the forms of inequality, injustice in health care is the most shocking and inhumane.' It is inexcusable that more than five decades later, health care is still inaccessible to a huge number of people in our country.

Of course, it's easy to criticize those in power and drop quotes like, 'Our health-care system is neither healthy nor cares, and it is no system in the first place.' The question really is: Why don't you and I do something about it?

'Let us be the ones who say we do not accept that a child dies every three seconds simply because he does not have the drugs you and I have. Let us be the ones to say we are not satisfied that your place of birth determines your right for life.

Let us be outraged, let us be loud, let us be bold,' urged the Hollywood actor Brad Pitt.

What I'd say is, brother, if we're really bold, let's do something about it. Being loud isn't enough, being a doer is a more emphatic statement to make. And that's what my team and I set out to do when we were confronted by hordes of human beings who had serious health problems but couldn't get a foot in the door to get curative help.

One doesn't have to be a medical practitioner to realize that a health issue is exacerbated by stress. And what greater stress can there be when, apart from illnesses, people face a severe financial strain too?

The road to good health should be paved with good intentions. But we knew that we were not a team of doctors who could extend pro-bono services. A self-appraisal led us to believe that what we could do was to at least try and take the stress caused by the unaffordability and inaccessibility of health care out of people's lives.

Thus, the app Ilaaj India, which translates to 'Cure India', came into existence in September 2020.

Once we embarked on our humanitarian mission, appeals for help started coming at us in unmanageable numbers and different forms. A few weeks into our mission, we discovered that one consistent plea, growing in alarming numbers, was for assistance in a multitude of health-related matters. Financial help was one part of it; the other part had to do with attracting the attention of health-care workers for patients without a voice. These patients needed medication, they needed medical intervention, and they needed procedures and operations. What started off as a random distress call from someone requiring surgery slowly led to many more, until it became impossible for us to cope with them in a conventional manner.

Initially, we took each as a stray case and went about it without an organized plan. We didn't stop to calculate just how long-drawn the process was to get medical aid for a person. I had to call hospitals for beds and simultaneously call surgeons, seeking their expertise and time. I had to open accounts with chemists at hospitals or near the homes of the patients, to ensure uninterrupted medical supplies for every patient.

And then it became physically impossible to do this in the personal, traditional way. Word spreads when help and hope are available. After all, health gives hope and hope is what makes the world go around.

But we were unprepared. The appeals snowballed. From a request or two a day, it became twenty per day, and before we knew it, we were faced with an avalanche. When it came rolling down bigger and faster, we knew that we could no longer handle it case by case. Health was a major concern that touched everybody, and it called for a permanent, professional approach. We had to start with a study and move to quick solutions.

Could we as a small team of like-minded people driven by the common desire to alleviate the pain of the underprivileged help to make a difference? 'Never believe that a few caring people can't change the world. For, indeed, that's all who ever have,' said the author and anthropologist Margaret Mead.

We believed that the least we could do was to make a concerted effort. So we put our heads together and came up with Ilaaj India, an app to connect people seeking medical help with those equipped to provide it to them.

In my six-month 'discovery of India', I found there were hundreds of people who couldn't afford basic health care. In such situations, more advanced medical attention was out of the question. I had people arriving at my doorstep from as far as Andhra Pradesh, Telangana, Tamil Nadu, Karnataka, Uttar Pradesh and other states—all of them seeking medical aid. There were parents carrying sick children in their arms who beseeched my team for financial assistance and access to treatment.

When we were arbitrarily stepping in to provide help to individuals, we had arranged for several people to be treated where they lived or at places closest to them. There were many surgeries organized by my team and me, but when the numbers rose, we sat down and worked out a long-term solution to provide help to those who desperately needed it.

The need was for a platform to connect patients with doctors and hospitals. We worked on Ilaaj India at a breakneck pace. I was personally on the job as I spoke to countless doctors from various medical disciplines and got a commitment from them that they would do a minimum of one free surgery every month for the rest of their lives.

Winston Churchill said, 'We make a living by what we get, but we make a life by what we give.' Doctors and surgeons made a living with their skills. They were now ready to make a life by giving their skills, just once a month, without handing out bills at the end of it.

Within weeks, I got around 50,000 doctors and surgeons from all over India on board. They gave us assurance that they would join hands with Ilaaj India and perform one free surgery every month, for as long as they were able to.

What has been a wonderful revelation is the willingness of so many medical experts who gave me their word that they would offer their services and time for free to strangers they were yet to meet. Once again, I bow to the Almighty for giving me the fame that works as a key that opens so many doors.

Fortunately, Ilaaj India could take off also because Digital India has grown rapidly, making the use of smartphone apps possible in the remotest parts of the country.

Once it was worked out, it was simple. Now, a patient in, say, Gorakhpur, who needs medical help of any kind, can get on to our Ilaaj India app and upload his case study along with whatever supporting documents he has. For our part, we peruse the details and map out the appropriate surgeons or specialists across India who are available to take care of that particular case. Once the right doctor is approached, other facilities, like a hospital bed, are fixed up, and we keep our fingers crossed, hoping that the patient in Gorakhpur gets his treatment at the earliest.

Ilaaj India aims to get the patient the best possible help in the shortest possible time and at the closest possible venue. We strive to get the surgeries or procedures done at hospitals easily accessible to patients. But we can also make arrangements to get them treated in bigger metros like Mumbai or Delhi, depending on the immediacy and the kind of time the patient has.

On 24 September 2020, RepublicWorld.com reported, 'Bollywood actor and philanthropist Sonu Sood has recently launched the *"Ilaaj India"* initiative. The aim of the initiative is to extend support for medical care and treatment of children. *Ilaaj India* is a helpline number initiative that is aimed to bridge the affordability gap and make health care accessible to everyone. Any patient who is in need to undergo any medical treatment can give a missed call at the helpline and the organisation will help patients arrange financial support for them to undergo any kind of medical treatment or critical surgeries.'

Ilaaj India has already expanded beyond paediatrics; it is now available to all age groups.

For me, Ilaaj India was born when I learnt of the magnitude of the health-care problem that afflicts thousands of Indians. The figures shook me: an unbelievable number of children died due to inadequate medical attention in 2019. It was a number that was startlingly higher than that recorded in any other developing country. The problem became more vivid as I also realized that there is an inadequate number of government hospitals in our country to accommodate the growing number of patients. The stress on both hospitals and patients is disturbing and has to be resolved.

In addition to the shortage of well-equipped nursing homes and medical centres, the limited coverage of health insurance forces people who can't afford good health care to dip into their own pockets to avail private health-care services. It is a burden that most people can't carry through their lifetime.

The Ilaaj India helpline number was established to ease this burden and provide patients with financial aid for medical treatment and surgery.

It is 020–67083686.

A missed call to this number activates the Ilaaj India team, which then reaches out to the patient and takes it from there. The app helps provide support to patients requiring medical care and treatment, which includes transplants or any critical surgery.

My dream is to make medical help available to as many needy patients as we can, and it's a boon that Ilaaj India has received widespread media attention. As *Goa Chronicle* published, '*Ilaaj India*, a helpline number initiative, is launched with an endeavour towards bridging the affordability gap and making quality healthcare accessible to all.'

'To all' is right, for Ilaaj India has already become a global philanthropic campaign, set up to provide medical services for free or at minimal rates to the extremely needy and destitute across India and around the world. It will direct the attention of a worldwide chain of doctors, surgeons and medical practitioners towards those who need their hands-on, specialized experience. And to ensure that only the genuine cases reach the medical experts, the patients are routed to them through the Sood Charity Foundation.

Before an empanelled medical practitioner is connected with a patient, the Sood Charity Foundation appraises, verifies and checks for the accuracy, authenticity and validity of each case. So all referrals are vetted and filtered by the foundation and only the selected ones reach the health-care experts.

The work I've got involved in has led me to also make some alterations in my life. Let me quote the health counsellor Toni Sheppard: 'A healthy attitude is contagious but don't wait to catch it from others. Be a carrier.' On a lighter note, this is the only kind of carrier one must be through life.

I've decided to be a carrier and spread my 'attitude' in every way I can. One way is to reserve my limited time and presence to associate only with platforms and brands that step up and contribute to the amelioration of suffering in the world. I tell people unequivocally, 'I will come and speak at your webinar only if you use your platform to come forward and do some genuine good.' In this manner, 200 surgeries have been performed through barter. So this is my new pitch: 'I will turn up for you if you in exchange do the world a good turn.'

I have found that you have to spread the 'contagion' of service for it to catch on. You have to vocalize what you're doing and what you'd like others to do too. It is pragmatic to manoeuvre your strength into pursuits which benefit society. It's a clear message I send out: 'Please use your resources, your brand name and my association with you for a larger common good.'

Sitting back and hoping that people will have a magical change of heart and volunteer their services is akin to living in a fool's paradise. A noble intent has to translate into action to achieve societal transformation. You have to reach out, pick up the phone and make those calls. Each one of us is capable of moving a stone, if not a mountain. Remove the stones, lift the hurdles and work towards a social goal. Change happens. I, Sonu Sood of 2020, stand testimony to it.

Through Ilaaj India I have attempted to make India healthier; my effort has been to connect India medically and emotionally. You and I protect our own with insurance policies and medical aid that's available at our fingertips. But when it comes to taking care of the health of the nation, we tend to do it more in thought and less in deed. Vision cannot be a substitute for action. Ilaaj India is my attempt to do more each day.

'The best way to find oneself is to lose oneself in the service of others,' said Mahatma Gandhi. With Ilaaj India, I have found a little more of myself.

7

UN Boosts the Brand

I have always felt that an honour is not a gift; you have to earn it.

The evening of 29 September 2020 held a special hour for me when I quite unexpectedly joined the outstanding ranks of Angelina Jolie, David Beckham, Leonardo DiCaprio, Emma Watson and Liam Neeson. What did I have in common with all these wholesome household names except that we were all actors?

It took my breath away when I received this in the mail (see inset).

I counted till ten and, for just a few seconds, felt a wee bit taller, now that I was a part of the league

of celebrities to be thus honoured by a body of the United Nations.

But soon it wasn't hubris but humility that engulfed me. The words of Calvin Coolidge, the thirtieth US President, echoed in my brain: 'No person was ever honoured for what he received. Honour has been the reward for what he gave.'

The citation from the UN seemed an extension of that sentence as it read: 'For selflessly extending a helping hand and sending home lakhs of migrants, helping thousands of stranded students across geographies abroad, providing free education and medical facilities to young children and creating free employment opportunities to the needy in the wake of the Covid-19 pandemic, Sonu Sood has been conferred the prestigious SDG (Sustainable Development Goals) Special Humanitarian Action Award by the United Nations Development Programme (UNDP).'

This exalted commendation came my way at a virtual ceremony on 29 September, adding a surprise feather to my simple *topi*. A recognition of this repute from the UN was unparalleled for me, not least because whatever little I have done for my fellow countrymen, in my own modest way, was without any expectations. I asked for and anticipated no returns, no rewards, except the feeling of fulfilment deep within me. However, to be recognized and awarded at an international forum does feel like a special blessing.

The SDGs, also known as the Global Goals, were adopted by all United Nations member states in 2015 as a universal call to action to end poverty, protect the planet and ensure that the whole world enjoys peace and prosperity by 2030.

It is a global vow that I wholeheartedly endorse and will be proud to live up to all my life.

It was a soul-stirring moment for me to take the pledge to 'Leave No One Behind', a commitment that UN member countries have made to think of those 'furthest behind first'. I really love that phrase; it is so overwhelmingly meaningful and appropriate.

The SDGs are designed to bring the world to a phase where there is zero poverty, hunger, illnesses like AIDS and discrimination against women and girls. The UNDP is doing exemplary work all over the world, and mankind will greatly benefit from the implementation of these goals. I am privileged to be officially kicking some of the winning shots towards those goals.

Although I didn't seek it, I acknowledge that the accolade from the UN goes beyond the recognition and rewards that I have received all these years as an actor. Showbiz is about being showy and larger than life; it's a world that gave me the name and fame to get things done. And acting is a profession that I will always love. But humanitarian work is the other end of the rainbow, the unassuming, down-to-earth phase of life where the true pot of gold awaits.

When you get national and international acclaim, when you go into a realm where few of your colleagues have reached and when you're catapulted into a position where you will be helping the UNDP to further the earth-saving cause of the SDGs, it makes you feel grateful and humble. I say this straight from the heart.

A natural but totally uncalculated bonus is the boost that all these achievements have given my brand equity. I'll let the headline of an opinion piece by Carol Goyal, published on 29 September in the *Economic Times*, say it all on my behalf: 'Brand Sonu Sood Stands Taller with UNDP Award'.

'In a celebrity world currently reeling under the impact of drug allegations, nepotism, suicide, murder, activism, politics and more, Sonu Sood has stood out in 2020 as a beacon of self-less service and humanitarian work that meaningfully impacted and benefited thousands, if not lakhs of migrants across geographies. Last night he received one of the biggest recognitions of his career: a UNDP award for Special Humanitarian work. Not only Sonu Sood, but each of us Indians, should celebrate the award which is a rare global honour for a job well done.

'For the record, Aishwarya Rai Bachchan, Shabana Azmi, Manisha Koirala, Dia Mirza and Lara Dutta have also been associated with the United Nations but they have been only Goodwill Ambassadors. Priyanka Chopra has similarly played Ambassador both in India and abroad. In a manner of speaking, Sonu, will be the only Bollywood male actor to have been awarded by UNDP. In the past, Amitabh Bachchan, Aamir Khan and Ayushmann Khurrana have done their bit for UNICEF but have not been recipients of a major UN Award.'

Posing the question 'What will this award do for Brand Sonu Sood?', she further analysed, 'Sonu has already been on a roll since the past few weeks with endorsements he has signed for MFine, SpiceJet, Acer, Pepsi, Edelweiss Insurance, IG International and more brands, that have lined up to sign the "Migrant Mahatma" as their ambassador. With Bollywood in turmoil, and with celebrity endorsements

under stress, the emergence of Sonu Sood as a messiah of
the poor and needy actually positions him as a top choice
for brands that profess to place the consumer and the
consumer's welfare ahead of profits and revenues. A client
I spoke to recently put it very nicely, "Sonu Sood gives
positive vibes. He comes across as sincere, and purpose-
driven. I want to trust him, believe in him. That is a very
important feeling when hiring a famous face."'

I am overwhelmed by this description. But I have to
accept that what I have been witnessing is a staggering
snowball effect. Consider this unaccountable series of events:
I become a celebrity face. I use this face, name and access
to help bring solace to those suffering, and benefit my
brethren. Internally, it gives me immense satisfaction; and
in the outside world, these acts of kindness, which I would
label as my duty as a human, fetch me unrivalled attention,
worldwide accolades and global awards, which push up my
brand equity. The boost in Brand Sonu Sood gives me a
unique place in the commercial market where endorsements
and campaigns follow. I use that for further societal good by
insisting that my brand association will come with the clause
that all these platforms will work towards the upliftment of
the underprivileged in one way or the other.

The year 2020 was when I began to sift through the stack
of offers and went into collaboration with different brands
to fund education, get surgeries performed, give homes to
the roofless, get their houses painted and bring dignity into
countless lives. For instance, when I began my association
with Shyam Steel, a leading metal brand known for TMT
bars, we embarked on making homes and exploring the

possibility of building 200 classrooms in schools that needed financial aid.

Similarly, I also started to politely turn down awards and asked hosts and event organizers to give me a reward instead. Reward as in, step forward and aid the surgery of a needy person. The Ilaaj India app is another example of that. With the medical fraternity by our side and hospitals across India taking an oath to offer us competitive rates and priority with beds and meds, we are the conduits; we'll help those who're in a position to help others.

My wardrobe doesn't need another shawl; my shelves aren't looking for another trophy. But my heart has a place to save another life. So, help me save another breadwinner; help me put them back on their feet so that they can take care of their families.

With Ilaaj India, we started with four surgeries, doubled the figure and then touched fourteen to sixteen surgeries a day. By the end of October, we had facilitated more than 600 operations all over India. Not a staggering number for sure, but please do the maths. If an individual's efforts could make that impact, which continues to grow every day, multiply it by all the brands and hosts who can join the bandwagon and see what happens.

It's a great place to be in. Commercial endorsements and ad campaigns are a part of the celebrity package today, and I embrace them. But to be able to go beyond market value and urge brands to have a societal orientation and commitment is so much more fulfilling.

Whatever acclaim I get, I turn it around to further assist the world. For instance, I know that I've received unprecedented media coverage for the work I have been doing, right from the time the first bus was whistled off on 15 April 2020. But more than an ego massage for myself, the coverage has instead given a fillip to every bit of social work that I have been engaged in. Without this nationwide dispersal of information spotlighting my mission, every official and authority I reached out to wouldn't have heartily agreed to cut out the red tape to help the migrants. Without the public cheering, my Pravasi Rojgar Yojna (which I will come to later) wouldn't have helped nearly half a million blue- and grey-collar workers find employment. My Ilaaj India project would not have found so many willing volunteers from the medical community, offering free consultations, treatment and surgeries.

Converting popularity into philanthropy is a win-win for all.

On this exhilarating ride, I have been asked if my fast drive in the humanitarian lane will make me switch to screen roles of the do-gooder. I place my bets on the American writer Walter Lippmann's wisdom: 'He has honor if he holds himself to an ideal of conduct.' So intent and conduct matter above all else and bring honour.

I believe that the audience can smartly distinguish between the two halves of an actor's life. If Sunil Dutt played a dacoit on screen, it didn't come in the way of his off-camera path of peace and brotherhood. At the same time, I'm forty-seven; I have the time to change tracks—if that's what the Almighty wills. I leave it, as always, to the Great Puppeteer.

8

Leg Up for Chennai Cook

Name: Bhonu Laal
Age: Twenty-eight
Profession: Domestic cook
Evacuated from: Chennai
Destination: Mirzapur, Uttar Pradesh
Reason: Father's accident

Day one was 15 April 2020. It began with 350 migrants who'd been shipwrecked in Mumbai getting a smooth sail home. Four months into the pandemic, the Ghar Bhejo initiative changed the lives of over 90,000 Indians scattered all over the globe.

I often sit up in disbelief at what we have achieved together. I began as a celebrity voice who had the means to bring some light into the lives of the utterly helpless. But now, there are nights when I lie awake, trying to figure out how and when a determined resolve turned into an overwhelming, nationwide campaign that spilt over and went beyond the shores of our country. Even as I write and while there is an 'un-lockdown' process being attempted, requests for a passage home continue to pour in from different parts of the world.

I'm just a well-intentioned man. When did I morph into a figure in whom people, who'd never met me before, could place their trust? What made a purposeful move turn into a mass movement? These thoughts of mine are juxtaposed with the innumerable memories collated over the months. I have a pile of photographs and video clips, real-life visuals and on-the-ground conversations, messages and emails, every possible medium of communication that has made me a part of the families of the masses of people who were total strangers to me until yesterday. Team Ghar Bhejo and I have received gratitude and thank-yous that defy counting.

In the midst of such a flood of human stories, some stand out as vivid for the extraordinary vulnerability of the people involved. They make you pause at the dinner table and wonder why misery cannot be wiped out as marks on a blackboard with a duster. If only I'd been gifted with such an eraser. Among the few such stories that have stayed at the forefront of my memory is the case of Bhonu Laal from Mirzapur, Uttar Pradesh.

Bhonu is a twenty-eight-year-old domestic cook, the only earning member of his large family. Besides his ageing parents, he has two brothers and four sisters, making it a family of nine.

He worked as a cook in the house of a Marwari gentleman miles away from Mirzapur, in Chennai. Earning a monthly salary of about Rs 7500, he was happy with the family he lived with and worked for. He'd been in their employ for quite a few years, and since his family depended on him for their survival, he would send home most of his income. Most young men in his situation are reconciled to the idea of living from day to day, with no savings to speak of. As long as nobody had to worry about his next meal, there were no complaints.

It's really heart-rending to find how so many people are grateful just to have enough to eat every day, with little thought given to the future. Bhonu was one of those faceless millions.

At the beginning of the lockdown, just when all the state borders were closed in India and movement became almost impossible, Bhonu received news from home that shattered him. His father, Salik Ram, who used to make a living in his younger days by selling pottery, had met with an accident. The lean senior citizen, dressed in a cream-coloured kurta pyjama as on most days, had gone for a walk. But on that fateful day, when he was attempting to cross the railway tracks, he failed to hear the train speeding towards him. By the time he jumped to save himself, the train had run over one of his legs, which was lost within seconds.

When the news reached Bhonu, his family wanted him to come home immediately. And Bhonu wanted to be with his father and his family at a trying time like this. But during the lockdown in Chennai, to even dream of a passage home was impossible for the young man. Bhonu was in sheer despair.

I received a photograph of Bhonu's father, whose leg had been amputated, along with Bhonu's plea for help. This was a person who required a sympathetic ear and immediate relief.

I spoke to him personally, and he wept as he explained his plight to me over the phone. I assured him that I'd do my best for him. It meant putting him on a flight out of Chennai and making arrangements for him to reach home.

Fortunately, a few flights had started operating between the bigger metros, and I could ensure that Bhonu caught a Chennai-to-Allahabad (via Delhi) flight the very same evening. I could empathize with him because I know how the heart flutters when something so terrible happens to a parent while you are miles away.

When Bhonu reached home before nightfall on the next day and met his father, he was inconsolable. But he was also very grateful that he could be with his family at such a time, and his 'thank you' came with a photograph of his father and him.

The sad story of Bhonu Laal was something I couldn't forget. There were many follow-ups with him. When I spoke to him a few days later, he was at the dispensary with his father. It was gratifying for me that a son could be by his father's side when the family needed him. As I always say, I am only the facilitator.

One could question why Bhonu had to leave his job in Chennai when his steady income would have helped the family more than his presence in Mirzapur. But it was a sorry state of affairs out there.

Bhonu's older brother, who suffers from epilepsy, himself required treatment and care. He couldn't possibly have helped his parents during his father's medical travails. His younger brother is a school-going lad, too young to shoulder his family's responsibility. A ray of light was that all his four sisters are married and their husbands contributed whatever little they could to help the family in distress. But Bhonu's brothers-in-law had their own worries, since they too were finding it impossible to make ends meet during the pandemic.

There was stress on all sides. With Bhonu having left Chennai and his job, his parents, his two brothers and he himself now had virtually nothing to survive on. He, who had made a living for the better part of his younger days by rustling up and serving hot meals to the family he worked for, was now in a state where he couldn't feed his own family and couldn't afford the bare essentials.

Apart from the basic expenses required for the family's survival, his father's medical expenses were burning an additional hole in his pocket. While it gave me satisfaction that I could expedite and ensure a quick journey for Bhonu to be with his father during a medical emergency, his financial woes became my worry.

But there is a limit to what one can do. Besides, the idea is not to make them all dependent on one source. The long-term vision is to get such people a stable means of livelihood so that they can stay with their families and take care of them. Yet it is not always possible for my team and me to achieve the goal of not only getting the migrants home but also easing their financial burden.

Until the pandemic is fully under control, our main focus will be on getting people home. Making them stand on their own feet, 'Naukri Dilao', get them jobs, will be the next leg of Ghar Bhejo.

As I've been saying all these months, I'm not really equipped to do what we have done. But every time a new challenge comes up, Team Ghar Bhejo gets back to the drawing board, burns the midnight oil, puts on its thinking cap and puts in the hard work to come up with a workable solution.

In Bhonu's case too, I'm confident, we shall overcome.

'Sonu Sood came into my berangi (colourless) life as a ray of hope. He not only united me with my family when my father lost his leg; he also inquired about our well-being throughout for the last few months of our acquaintance. Even today, I sometimes send him messages and videos because he's like a lifeline I'm clutching on to in these extraordinarily trying times. Every day, strife keeps me busy, but I keep wondering— will I ever make it to Mumbai to see Sonu Sir in the flesh? It's a thought that keeps me motivated.'

—Bhonu Laal

9

An Off-Camera Shot

Name: Surendra Rajan
Age: In his eighties
Work: Film artiste
Problem: Unemployment, depression, loneliness
To be fetched from: A Mumbai suburb
Destination: Panna, Madhya Pradesh

Recall Maqsood Bhai, the hospital staffer who gets a *jadoo ki jhappi* from Sanjay Dutt, in *Munna Bhai M.B.B.S.*? That's Surendra.

Have you ever worked amicably with a senior without ever getting to know him? And then one day he re-enters your life poignantly? I got this experience on this trek of service to others that I have undertaken.

Shooting for the film *R . . . Rajkumar* (2013) had gone off uneventfully. One of my co-actors in it was Surendra Rajan-ji, a senior character actor in his early eighties who has done innumerable films. Other than *Munna Bhai M.B.B.S.,* he has marked his presence in films like *Veer Savarkar* (2001), *The Legend of Bhagat Singh* (2002) with Ajay Devgn, and *Bose: The Forgotten Hero* (2004) among several foreign-language projects that he has been a part of.

'Sometimes life hits you in the head with a brick. Don't lose faith.' Easier said than done, I'd say to Steve Jobs. But the thought expressed by the founder of Apple does explain what happened to Surendra.

Surendra's hometown is in Madhya Pradesh. Whenever he had an assignment, he'd come and stay in a matchbox-sized rented apartment in a distant Mumbai suburb. He came to Mumbai for a web series in early 2020, when the unsparing pandemic and ensuing lockdown threw him off balance. Life had hit him in the head with a brick.

Grey-haired Surendra-ji was stuck in that tiny apartment all by himself. His family and friends were back home in Madhya Pradesh, and he was here on his own. Two months into the lockdown, it was like he'd been put in solitary confinement. For a man who was eighty-plus, this must have been unbearable.

There was no work happening, his money was running out and worst of all, he had no one for company. It wasn't as if he hadn't tried to go back to Madhya Pradesh. He had made several aborted attempts to leave Mumbai by train or bus. But he couldn't manage to find transport that could take him to Panna district, where his hometown was located.

Two months into the lockdown, Surendra-ji had started to fear that he may lose his mind. He felt constricted and claustrophobic, and loneliness is a hard cross to carry at any age. More so in one's eighties, during a social lockdown.

With the money dwindling, there was the additional worry of how he'd pay his monthly rent. He told me his landlord was kind and was ready to give him a waiver for a couple of months. But for all of us, our dignity is the armour we wear. We don't want pity beyond a point. Whichever way he turned, he saw only an impregnable wall.

Finally, he reached out to me through common acquaintances and introduced himself as my co-actor in *R. . . Rajkumar*. Of course, that wasn't necessary. I knew who he was; I knew him as a well-known senior actor.

The pandemic had truly spared no one. When I heard Surendra-ji's story, I told him almost immediately that I would do my utmost to get him to his home in Madhya Pradesh.

Soon, we were able to put together a vehicle that would drive him from his apartment in Mumbai to his doorstep in Madhya Pradesh. We could top it off with additional funds required for his journey.

Surendra-ji was ecstatic.

In Mumbai, he'd spent long weeks of dependence on the kindness of his neighbours and acquaintances. Since he lived alone, he desperately sought the company of others to come and chat with him. He also needed the occasional hot meal.

It was a new kind of hardship for him, because when life was normal, in the pre-coronavirus days, he would have been out of his house and among colleagues on a bustling film set. He had company, he had food, work and money in his pocket. He was well cared for in normal times.

However, the pandemic had not only deprived him of his livelihood but also of his dignity to some degree, because he was actually asking people to come and be around him. Nobody would want that kind of dependence on their acquaintances.

After reaching a friend's farmhouse in Panna, he felt exhilarated and could finally breathe freely. It was as if the shackles had come off. He could move around unhindered and unfettered. He called me up from there to inform me that he had got into a wonderful routine of going on long walks in the wilderness around his friend's farmhouse. Wherever he looked, he saw greenery, he said over a phone call. This made me happy. I was genuinely relieved, because I worried about his physical and mental well-being.

He also spoke passionately about how he was able to do some sketching. Surendra-ji is one of those rare talents who is both an artiste and an artist.

It was only when I heard the happiness in his voice during that phone call, and sensed the freedom he felt once he was out of that apartment in Mumbai, that I understood how important space was for a human being, especially for elders. He absolutely loved the open spaces that welcomed him back home in Madhya Pradesh. From fearing that he was getting unhinged to chuckling with delight, Surendra-ji was a changed man.

It touched me when I got to know that he'd told many people, 'I've seen many caped heroes—Superman, Batman, Spiderman, etc. But believe me, Sonu is the first real hero I have encountered in my life. What he did for me during this pandemic is something I can't thank him enough for.

It's odd. He is so much younger than I am, yet in my eyes, he showed more maturity than I myself would have. I will even go to the extent of saying that he came like an angel into my world and literally rescued me from going downhill mentally and physically. God bless him.'

I do feel blessed, every single day.

I cannot express the immense joy I felt at being able to provide timely help to such a senior colleague. In our recent conversations, Surendra-ji has often reminded me of how little we'd interacted while shooting *R...Rajkumar*. And he has repeated many a time that he had never imagined that this was how our paths would cross. But that's life.

I also feel that when life gets fast-paced again, which it will post the pandemic, I will always remind myself to take a few moments off to spend time with the seniors I encounter on sets. Perhaps a little kindness will go a long way in making someone's day.

10

The Stamp of a Champ

Name: Amritpal Kaur
Age: Twenty-three
Profession: Karate
Place: Delhi
Reason: Knee surgery

'Alone we can do so little, together we can do so much.'
I endorse American author Helen Keller's words because I'm a
team player, as every captain should be. Perhaps it stems from
my love for sports. If I didn't have a passion for acting, I would
have been out there in the field chasing a dream career in cricket.

But since I opted for a studio instead of a stadium, acting
became my profession and cricket a pastime. Cricket was a
childhood choice, my favourite game. Even after I grew up
and chose make-up and make-believe over bat and ball, my
fondness for sports has remained, and I'm always linked in
some way or the other with it. Four years ago, I was happy

to be named the face of the Delhi team in the Pro Kabaddi League. Kabaddi is another team game that gives me an adrenaline rush.

Now, as a parent, it gives me a thrill to find that my younger son, Ayaan, who is eleven years old, has shown a gift for cricket at a very young age. I have vowed to nurture his natural flair for the game and make him a professional cricketer. In the compound of our building, I have laid out a green patch for net-practice sessions, where I encourage all the neighbourhood kids to come and play with Ayaan. I have also hired a coach, who comes to our building to train the children who're genuinely interested in the game.

I unabashedly admit that it gives me the chance to indulge in my childhood passion as I join the kids for a round of cricket whenever I can. Of course, Ayaan beats me at the game, which actually makes me a rather proud father.

It gladdens me because sports are not only about winning or losing a game. They equip you to play well in any field. Fitness, focus, drive, determination, rigorous practice, utter professionalism and team spirit will give you victory in any arena.

'Teamwork is the ability to work together toward a common vision. The ability to direct individual accomplishments toward organizational objectives. It is the fuel that allows common people to attain uncommon results.' I'd like to believe that Andrew Carnegie's observation sums up the success and growth of Mission Ghar Bhejo, which has gone far beyond a campaign for sending migrants home.

Just the other day, a young girl named Sweta Singh tweeted to me saying she couldn't get a room in a Patna hospital for her father-in-law, who had tested positive for the coronavirus. And within that day, we spoke to the right authorities and arranged for his hospital stay.

As I've been saying since 15 April 2020, I'm here for the long haul. Ghar Bhejo was only the springboard for my team and me, so we could commit ourselves to the service of others in every way we can.

Against this backdrop of teamwork and sports, let me present to you the story of a unique opportunity we got to save one of our country's brightest sportswomen during the COVID-19 lockdown.

One morning, I woke up to a message from someone called Anmol Singh. I didn't know him, but he introduced himself as a friend of the karate champion Amritpal Kaur.

Amritpal is a part of the national karate team and has represented our country at several international championships. Her achievements have been spectacular. She won a gold medal at the eighth Commonwealth Karate Championships in 2015. She brought home a bronze at the Asian Karate Federation Championships in 2018. She is also a three-time gold medallist at the South Asian Karate Championships.

I would unhesitatingly call Amritpal the pride of our country, because to me, all sportspersons who put India on the world map need a salute. One must care for them, respect them and encourage them. And you already know about my close affinity with women achievers since my childhood.

The message from Amritpal's friend went on to inform me that our champ had injured her knee during the KAI President Cup 2020, held in Goa on 8 January, just before the pandemic. (KAI stands for the Karate Association of India.)

To paraphrase Sylvester Stallone's line from *Rocky Balboa*, 'It isn't about how hard you can kick. It's about how hard you can *get* kicked, and keep moving forward.' Amritpal exemplified this champ mindset. Despite her injury, in the true never-give-up spirit of a sportsperson, Amritpal continued with her practice sessions, which ended up causing more damage to her knee. Now, she was in agony.

The medical team that examined her recommended immediate surgery, because of third-degree damage to her anterior cruciate ligament, one of the two ligaments that are in the centre of the knee.

But due to financial constraints, Amritpal wasn't able to get herself the required treatment. She is the youngest in an economically backward family, and it was impossible for her folks to put together enough to meet her medical costs. Amritpal had turned to the Sports Federation and the relevant ministry for support. But for reasons best known to them, the authorities didn't respond in time, and in mid-March the country went into a lockdown. It compounded her misery, not only leading to a delay in her surgery but also adding to her financial worries.

She was in excruciating pain and couldn't afford the surgical intervention that she needed to back on her feet. Her plight touched me. I would have never imagined that one of India's leading lights in sports would also have to bear the brunt of the COVID-19 pandemic.

Amritpal is no quitter. She approached every avenue possible to raise funds, even decided to try crowdfunding. But everywhere she turned, she bumped into a brick wall—she got no response from any quarter, nothing was working out.

What worked was her undying determination. It was like she was out to *uke* (the word for 'block' in karate) any attempts to thwart her. And she was going to *zuki*, punch her way out of her troubles.

Even in the state she was in, the ambitious girl was looking at finding a place for herself in the World Championships (that ultimately got postponed due to the lockdown). Tapping every resource she could, she got one of her friends to reach out to me on my Twitter timeline.

I heard from them on 8 July, and from my subsequent interactions with her, I soon learnt that she had actually taken a loan to represent India at the Asian Championships because our government didn't offer any support to these athletes. Underprivileged, a sportsperson and a woman achiever—it touched all the emotional buttons in me and I decided to step in.

I took to Twitter and asked her not to worry. She was a champion of our country, and life wasn't being fair to her. Once I took her case in hand, I assured Amrit and her family that she would spring back into action really soon and that they would have to look no further than me for her medical expenditure. For me, it was truly an honour to be able to extend a helping hand to a meritorious sportswoman like her.

My team shared her reports with a medical team in Delhi. Since she lived in Tilak Nagar in New Delhi, we also got a local doctor there to study and assess her case. On 12 July, I arranged for an ambulance, which fetched her from her residence the next day and drove her to Yatharth Hospital in Greater Noida, where she was admitted.

The operation to set her knee right was scheduled for 14 July. After undergoing the prescribed pre-surgery tests from 4 a.m. onwards, she was wheeled into the operating theatre at 8.30 a.m., and she went under the knife at 9 a.m. I'm detailing the whole process because we were mentally with her all the time and waited as anxiously as her family did. At 11.20 a.m., we whooped with joy and relief when the doctors came out and announced that the surgery was a success.

She's still to heal and recover completely. But she will soon be on the mat, punching and kicking her way into international championships.

I love this quote from Simone Arianne Biles, the American gymnast: 'I'm not the next Usain Bolt or Michael Phelps. I'm the first Simone Biles.' I'd say that for Amrit too. She's not the next anybody else. She is herself; she is Amritpal Kaur, a super fighter.

Hard-pressed financially, finding no support from the federation or the ministry, but never accepting defeat, Amrit is in the great company of names like Mary Lou Retton, another American gymnast, who once said, 'Erase the word "failure" from your vocabulary. No case is ever truly closed, and no challenge is ever over.'

The challenges will always be there for Amritpal. But, as wrestler Dan Gable said, 'Gold medals aren't really made of gold. They're made of sweat, determination, and a hard-to-find alloy called guts.' Amrit has them all.

Hers is a fascinating case. And once again, I felt blessed that I could play a part in this champion's story.

'I'm at home in Delhi, recouping after my knee operation. It is only a matter of months before I start participating in international karate championships. I promise to bring home a gold medal next summer. This one will be for India and for Sonu Sir. I'm indebted to him forever.'

—Amritpal Kaur

11

National Goes International

Name: Too many to list
Description: Labourers/patients/students/seniors
Countries to be evacuated from: Canada, Cyprus, Georgia, Kyrgyzstan, Kazakhstan, Philippines, Russia and Uzbekistan
Destination: Various cities in India
Reason: Stranded without work/shelter/funds
Date: Through the pandemic months

Main akela hi chala tha janib-e-manzil magar
Log saath aate gaye aur karwaan banta gaya

I feel as if poet and wordsmith Majrooh Sultanpuri gazed into the future and spotted me when he penned those words. I did indeed set out on my own towards my destination, but as people kept joining me en route, it unwittingly grew into a caravan.

That's precisely how I feel about that significant moment on 15 April, when Ghar Bhejo, a well-intentioned domestic campaign facilitated between states within the country, shaped into a gargantuan international operation. As the requests and cries for help came to me from all directions and distances, and called my attention to a whole new range of situations, many more people, including officials and authorities, became part of the ever-growing 'karwaan'.

'Growth is never by mere chance; it is the result of forces working together,' said James Cash Penney Jr, founder of the vast American department store chain J.C. Penney. In the case of Ghar Bhejo, the forces have been incalculable.

Like the migrant worker Prashant Kumar Pradhan, who set up a shop in Odisha and named it Sonu Sood Welding Work Shop, I too seemed to have opened an NGO outlet named 'Sonu Sood One-Stop Counter'. Our team began to resemble a phalanx of private branch exchange operators, receiving, messaging, connecting, coordinating, cajoling and consoling too. There were as many temperaments to be handled as there were requests. So it called for a team that could go beyond robot-like efficiency; the human touch was just as imperative.

A student tweets to me asking for textbooks, and I have them delivered to his/her doorstep the next day. Someone needs blood, another needs medical attention, and the buck stops at my counter. I, we, get it done. That's the kind of network we've systematically set up over the last four months. 'Come to me, I'm here to lighten your burden.'

As I always acknowledge with gratitude, this has been possible only because of my fame as a film star and the widespread attention my work has received. It has translated, inexplicably, into strangers placing their faith in me, which is touching, frightening and overwhelming on occasion!

It's a challenge to live up to the expectations of people reaching out to me with such hope.

The story of how I brought home 4000 students from Kyrgyzstan and another planeload from Uzbekistan spread so fast and so far that we started getting many more pleas to airlift students from elsewhere in the world. And the requests didn't come just from students.

In July 2020, when parents of over a hundred kids beseeched me to airlift their children from Moscow and ferry them to Chennai, I was caught off balance. Chennai was under complete lockdown, there were no flights going in or flying out. It was an insurmountable difficulty because when a state is under lockdown, you can't procure landing permissions. But the parents were desperate. Referring to Kyrgyzstan, they urged me to help them, saying that if I could pull off that feat, I could surely bring their children home too.

Most of them were medical students stranded in and around Moscow. I was pleasantly surprised to learn that so many of our Indian students went to universities in Russia and neighbouring countries. One of the things I did was to speak to the hundred-odd kids on a Zoom call. All of them said in unison, 'Sonu Sir, please get us out of here.' The feeling was, there's nothing *namumkin*, impossible; Sonu'll get it done. That kind of faith can perhaps move mountains.

On 5 August, they did land in Chennai, all the way from Moscow. I had managed to get last-minute permissions from the authorities in Moscow and Chennai to facilitate this journey of the medical students.

We had opened up the international skies earlier as well, when a student succumbed to COVID-19 in Kyrgyzstan.

His death created panic among the other Indian students, who wanted me to rescue them and couldn't wait to get away from there. Abhishek, a student from Bihar, took on the role of the lead spokesperson and liaised with me on behalf of the entire group. The fear of the pandemic had gripped them badly, and they wanted to cling on to someone, find a way out. When all the avenues and sources they tapped didn't translate into positive action, I was their last port of call. In fact, some of the students were stranded at a place that was twelve hours away from Kyrgyzstan and they too needed to be flown to safety. Likewise, the students in Uzbekistan, Kazakhstan and Moscow. Coming from different directions, they had to gather at one airport.

I didn't know how to handle an international evacuation. But did I want to step forward into uncharted territory and grow further, or step back into my comfort zone? One thing I knew for sure: that I wasn't going to step back even an inch. To move forward, I had to do what I hadn't attempted so far. Once again, I had to understand the mission, go back to the drawing board and plan how to do what I hadn't done before.

'Plan the work. Then work the plan.' American entrepreneur and industry leader Bob Antler put it so simply. I did just that.

My first move was to connect with the foreign embassies in all the countries from where messages for help had been received, and of course with the Ministry of External Affairs (MEA) in India. What energized me was the hearty response of the ambassadors of these countries as well as our officials at the MEA. What I heard was more or less unanimous—that since I had taken the initiative to help so many of these students and 'strandees' (a word we've coined), they in turn would help me with all the evacuation permissions as best and as quickly as they could. Once the hurdle of bureaucracy, red tape, permissions and procedures was crossed, coordination began to look a little less complicated.

The tough part was getting the first batch of students out. But once 1800 students from Kyrgyzstan had made it to India, the ensuing waves were easier to handle as a procedure had been set. The next group of 2200 arrived shortly after. That initial 4000 opened the floodgates as students from Canada, Georgia, Cyprus, Tashkent, Kazakhstan and the Philippines started to contact me on Twitter.

By the time the call for help came from Moscow, we were more or less geared to follow a certain procedure. But every evacuation poses its own unique challenges. In this particular case, Chennai being in complete lockdown was the challenge.

But the relief we felt when they arrived in Chennai on 5 August was well worth the efforts put in. We did some handholding post-arrival too, as we arranged discounted rates for all of them to be quarantined at various hotels in the city. It was clear that the students were happy to be on that plane. We saw photos of them beaming in their PPE kits on the flight; some were holding pictures of me. Sometimes, visuals speak better than words.

Dr T.R. Sakthi Priyadarshini, a graduate of the Kursk State Medical University in Russia, told the media, 'We were waiting for the Vande Bharat mission flight. Unfortunately, it was scheduled for a date before our final exams and graduation in July. We thought we could return during the subsequent phases of the mission, but there weren't any more flights from Russia to Chennai. We had our visas extended till 15 September, but we wanted to get back to India before the Foreign Medical Graduate Examination in August-end.'

That's when they reached out to me.

Another student, Dr Periyannan Somasundaram, elaborated, 'There was only one flight to Chennai, a 460-seater by a private operator. We didn't take it because we weren't sure of its reliability. We were around 180-plus students who wanted to reach Chennai from Russia, as flying through other cities could be risky.'

The young doctor said that he had mailed several government officials. And after reading about how I'd evacuated students from Kyrgyzstan, he mailed me too. Dr Somasundaram bluntly told interviewers in Chennai, 'None of them except Sonu Sir replied. I sent him a mail on 22 July, and I got his response the next morning. It took a few days to get the required permissions. Finally, by the time the flight was confirmed, there was only half the number of students. Yet, his team didn't cancel the flight. He had a video call with us a few days before the departure and assured us that we would be brought back.'

'We paid only for our tickets,' confirmed Dr Priyadarshini. 'The rest was taken care of by Sonu Sir and his team.'

Dr Somasundaram also said, 'He even arranged hotel rooms for us to be quarantined at, at cheaper rates. Also, on special request, one student was allowed to disembark in Delhi, when the aircraft halted for refuelling.'

All I would add to this is, Chennai, I'm so overjoyed that I could do this for your students. Because Chennai was where my star trek really began; Chennai was the city I reached by train, carrying with me a book called *How to Learn Tamil*; this was where I faced the camera for the first time for *Kallazhagar* as the wicked, bald villain opposite superstar Vijayakanth. I have a karmic connection with this bustling and lovely metropolis, and when students who hailed from here approached me for help, I had to respond to them and bring them home safely. I'd therefore say, *nandri*, Chennai, thank you, for giving me the opportunity to serve you. Being able to repay your karmic debts in your lifetime is also a blessing.

When students and professionals who were stranded in different parts of the globe started tagging me on social media asking for help, the first thought that popped into my mind was, 'How do I do this? I am not trained for it.'

'The minute you're satisfied with where you are, you aren't there any more.' I have to agree with the baseball star Tony Gwynn, as I too had to shake off complacence and go for more.

When so many people place their faith and hopes in you, the Almighty not only infuses you with an extra dosage of strength, He also lights up a path for you.

It was a strange feeling when students who were being offered alternative flight arrangements didn't consider them reliable and looked at me as a symbol of reassurance. They wanted to wait and see what arrangements my team and I could make for them. It became a question of trust, of the faith they had reposed in me. Most of them had followed the regular news briefs about the smooth evacuation of other student groups by Team Sonu Sood and waited for us to help them. Of course, it was odd that these youngsters were actually unwilling to wait even for the Vande Bharat flights and were ready to patiently stand in line for me to bring them home.

After 6 July there were no Vande Bharat flights scheduled, and the students weren't hopeful that one would be organized for them. There was also an August-end deadline for them to be back in Chennai in time for the Foreign Medical Graduate Examination. They were also willing to book their own tickets from any airport that would open up for them, but there were none. All airports were shut, so there was no question of tickets being issued. They even looked at chartering a flight, but permissions for it were not forthcoming from anybody.

After looking at all alternatives, the enterprising students then initiated communication with the PMO and the chief minister of Tamil Nadu. Hope was rekindled in them, and they cheered up when they got information that a private company was organizing a chartered flight on 18 July from Moscow to Chennai. It was super news for them, since most were from the south. When they looked expectantly at me, it put additional pressure on my team and on me; we had to ensure that every detail was worked out for them to touch terra firma in Chennai without a hitch.

That flight from Moscow to Chennai was nerve-racking for us. Apart from all other procedural formalities to be completed, the head count kept changing till the last minute, which made it almost impossible to get that plane off the ground. To initiate the rescue operation, it was imperative to get the exact roll call of the passengers, with accurate details. My team created a list on Google Forms as per government rules and circulated it among the students.

We got a total of 199 responses from different universities in Moscow, and we were good to go with these numbers for a chartered flight. Almost all of them belonged to south India, and as per quarantine rules, we had to send hotel and quarantine confirmations ahead of the flight landing in Chennai. It was manic. We were on the phone day and night, talking to embassy officials and to the ambassador, besides connecting with and updating the students on Zoom. They were an antsy bunch and were in touch with us on a daily basis to know the status and travel date. We arranged a hotel for them in Moscow while we completed the necessary formalities. It took a few days for all permissions to come through and for the final green signal to be flashed. But we finally set 5 August as the date of departure from Moscow.

One would think that we'd be entitled to a long-overdue sigh of relief after finalizing the date, but it was an ever-fluid situation. Two days before the departure, the numbers halved and only fifty-two seats were filled. It led to an expected panic among those fifty-two who wondered if we would cancel it if it came to flying a half-empty aircraft. At about 2 a.m., my team connected with me, and for the rest of the night, everybody sat up looking for other students who wished to return.

One source gave us a list of students from multiple universities who had not applied on our Google Forms but wanted to come back. We started calling them up and asking if they wanted to fly on 5 August from Moscow to Chennai. This time around, we had to gain their trust, because we were making random calls to students who hadn't reached out to us and asking them if they wanted to book tickets to get back home. Picture the chaos. On the one hand, we were talking to students who didn't know us and we were offering to bring them home. On the other, there were those fifty-two students who were continuously calling us, saying, 'Sir, please don't cancel this flight due to the reduced number. We'll be left helpless if you do that.' That was when I personally got on a Zoom chat with them to assure them that we would take off from Moscow on 5 August.

What we finally did was set up a conference call to connect this group of students, who'd already booked their tickets, with the other set, who needed to be convinced. We thus gained the trust of the new lot of students and more seats began to fill up. By the end of the day on 3 August, ninety-two seats had been booked, which was still woefully inadequate to fill a plane.

To solve this, an alternative we looked at was to approach SpiceJet and request them to arrange one halt at Delhi so that students who had homes in other states could also board our flight. Word came through from the airline, but we got radio silence from the Moscow end for the passengers to Delhi. Fortunately, the flight refuelled in Delhi and one student alighted there. When we finally flew out of Moscow on 5 August, we had 100 passengers on board, all headed for Chennai.

All through this period, I received personal messages from leaders of different student groups. In effect, what these messages said was, 'Sonu Sir, we know you will bring us home safe. Please do the best you can for us.'

When students place such blind trust in you because of the reputation you've earned as a man they can rely on, as a man who delivers, as a man who acts more than he speaks, you have to work with double the alacrity, integrity and responsibility. Students are the future of our country. I'm the father of two boys who're fast growing up. I have a seventeen-year-old at home, and I know what it means to win the faith of youngsters and watch out for them.

However formidable every task seemed when it first presented itself, we had a celestial hand over our heads as most of the evacuations went off practically glitch-free. In fact, our team followed up with most students to make sure that they not only reached their cities but also reached their homes safe and sound.

But it wasn't always smooth sailing. During our first massive international evacuation from Kyrgyzstan, we encountered a few unexpected roadblocks. But for every obstruction that came up, there was always hope on the horizon. I have to send out a special 'thank you, sir' to Alok Amitabh Dimri, India's ambassador to Kyrgyzstan. Initially, the simplest of requests, like basic permission to move students out, was not entertained. Everyone's first answer was always 'no' because of the fear of the disease. Every few steps, we got used to hearing words like, 'Pease do not encourage people to move around. They could be carriers of the virus or they can catch the infection. It is best to stay put where they are.' It took all my persuasion skills to get the students out of the different places and situations they were stuck in and bring them to India. It was a huge help, therefore, that whatever the issues, Mr Dimri provided us with enough assistance to sort them out.

Dr Phani Bhushan Potu, founder and president of ISM Edutech, one of the largest medical education hubs, and

Srinesh Vallabhaneni, CEO, ISM Edutech, helped my Ghar Bhejo team and me to evacuate students who were stuck in far-flung locations of Kyrgyzstan because of lack of transport during the pandemic. They worked alongside the Indian embassy members in Bishkek, Kyrgyzstan. Mr Dimri, too, played an instrumental role in making the process smoother for students to reach their homes in India. I must repeat that had it not been for all of these gentlemen, things would not have moved in the manner they did.

In Moscow, it was a repeat of the Kyrgyzstan situation. We managed to establish contact with Shipra Ghosh at the Indian embassy in Tashkent. Initially, perhaps because she wasn't conversant with our work, she seemed hesitant. What I was asking for must have also seemed like a crazy man's request. Who was this individual asking for help to evacuate 100-plus people from Moscow? But once Ms Ghosh realized the credibility and immediacy of our operation, and understood that it was about helping stranded students, she went out of her way to assist us. Without her, it wouldn't have been possible to achieve what we did.

During this amazing new journey, I was introduced to such a variety of people whom I've made new and warm associations with. In the Philippines, I spoke to Ambassador Mishra. I also spoke to Dondon Bagatsing, who worked at the embassy. His name has an interesting story behind it. It is adapted from the name of our Indian freedom fighter Shaheed Bhagat Singh. I discovered that Dondon is 25 per cent Punjabi. He got his surname from his father, who had immigrated to the Philippines and tweaked the spelling! He has still retained that Indian part of his name, but it is pronounced with an Anglicized twang and sounds cutely different.

Operation Manila turned out to be quite different from the other evacuations we had overseen so far. We discovered that over 100 people from the Philippines were also stuck in India and were waiting to head to their homes. On 7 August, approximately 180 passengers flew out of Mumbai and went to the Philippines and around 175 Indians arrived from Manila.

As I've remarked earlier, every operation came with its peculiar challenges. In the motley group of Indian passengers who flew back from the Philippines, there were also forty-odd patients with medical emergencies. Among them were people who had serious conditions, like requiring a liver transplant, but they had all been stuck in the Philippines because of the pandemic. Getting back such an assortment of people—including students and senior citizens—was a small triumph for us. For us, it was an intimidating assignment; for the people who came back on the chartered flight that we arranged for them, it was a miracle. Those who came to India for medical consultation were especially rapturous that I was able to bring them here. At one stage, they had almost given up all hope of reaching Indian shores.

Is it possible that I was instrumental in arranging to bring back people from places as diverse and as distant as Kyrgyzstan, Moscow and the Philippines? I sometimes feel like I'm in a trance and things are unfolding on their own, although I know that sweat, sincerity and sleepless nights have wrought them all.

While all these flights were being arranged for a cross section of Indians, I was on parallel lines working out plans to fly in people even from countries like Georgia and Canada. Every flight needed meticulous groundwork, as official permissions were required at every turn.

Besides the medical students from Moscow, I also brought home 108 labourers from Tashkent, Uzbekistan. They were a scattered bunch of abysmally poor people from various parts of Odisha, Jharkhand and Chennai. They were in no condition or position to come home on their own or to make any sort of arrangements for themselves. Had it not been for my teammates, who put wheels into motion to fly them home, these labourers would have had nowhere to go and no one to turn to. When I managed to talk to this group of migrants through a video conference, they were moved to see that their case had been heard by someone who cared. A few broke down in tears during the course of the call.

It was thus a continuous cycle that demanded non-stop pedalling. Once the first group of international evacuees came home successfully, there were innumerable demands registered on my timeline. People from different parts of the world were reaching out to us constantly, asking us to bring them home or to help them out of a desperate situation.

Even as we worked towards rescuing students stuck in different countries, we continued to deal with medical emergencies at home. One young girl in Uttar Pradesh was flying a kite and had her eye slashed by the *manja* (glass-coated string). She was on the verge of losing her eye. An SOS reached us. My team rushed to her rescue. Fortunately, she had already received the first round of medical aid. We diligently kept in touch with her and took updates on her condition.

At the Sonu Sood One-Stop Counter, I've received a host of messages asking me to provide wheelchairs and artificial limbs for the handicapped. My team got in touch with some leading manufacturers in Nagpur and got artificial limbs made for many who required them.

Each morning, for months on end, I've thought that perhaps I will now get a day to laze around and do nothing, catch up on sleep and rest body and mind. However, ever since the beginning of the pandemic and the lockdown, that day has never dawned. In fact, from April until now, I don't remember getting a proper night's rest. Each day brought me in close contact with a new human problem. It's a world of helpless, hapless people that I have entered, and I'm still standing at the rim. There are countless people looking for succour, and I don't see any of it coming to a halt anytime soon. It's been continuous and it's going to remain an unbroken chain, changing shape as we move along.

It is no longer just about Ghar Bhejo, for getting a migrant home doesn't mean the end of the journey; it is the beginning of a whole new set of problems. And service to mankind doesn't begin and end with migrant workers; there are scores of other people too who need help. When you spread your arms to embrace people, you realize that a sea of humanity awaits.

I said earlier that it was all somewhat frightening. But it's fascinating, too, to step back and see the unrecognizable figure I've turned into in just six months.

It sounds trite to say that the word 'impossible' may be read as 'I'm possible'. But it is true. And when the frightening 'impossible' is body-slammed, thrown to the ground and ticked off as 'project possible', the frightening transforms into the gratifying. The results are visible today. As Prime Minister Narendra Modi always says, 'Hard work never brings fatigue. It brings satisfaction.' I'm not fatigued.

With my friend Neeti Goel.

Karan Gilhotra.

The Sonu Sood
Department of Arts
and Humanities, at
the Sarat Chandra
IAS Academy in
Andhra Pradesh.

Residents of Kondapur village in the
Siddipet district of Hyderabad showed
their love for Sonu Sood by making a
statue in his likeness at a temple.

Team Ghar Bhejo

K.K. Mookhey.

Govind Agarwal.

Ashma.

Pankaj Jalisatgi.

Vishal Lamba.

Prashika Dua.

Ajay Dhama.

K.N. Karthikeyan.

Suchitra Laxman.

Ashu Tomar.

Chintan Desai.

Gautam and
Malvika Sachar.

Sumita Salve.

Janhvi and
Sidharth.

Amritpal Kaur, gold medallist in the Commonwealth Karate Championships, had trouble financing her surgery. So our team helped her out.

Amritpal Kaur after the surgery.

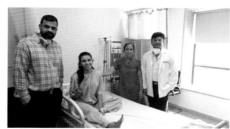

Our team's ration drive in Bihar.

Dashrath Manjhi's family.

Dubey-ji.

This is Komal, whom we rescued from Delhi along with her grandmother.

Abhishek Nagar, the student leader in Kyrgyzstan, on our first rescue flight out of the Central Asian country.

Praveen, Nagpur.

This man was among the thousands of stranded migrants in Bandra. He was happy to be going home and said to me, 'Sir, I was sure I was going to die here.'

Migrants at Bandra station.

Renu Barman, Assam.

Rita Viswakarma.

One of the men in Vasai, shortly before boarding the last train to Bihar. He said to me, 'I can't believe I got to meet the man who is sending me back home.'

Migrants on the train back home.

Bicycles were gifted to these girls in Mirzapur, who had to walk through a jungle in order to go to study.

Mallikarjun.

Nageswara Rao with his new tractor.

Warrior Aaji.

Harshwardhan.

Jalpaiguri, West Bengal.

The mobile tower in Morni, Haryana.

Prashant at his welding shop.

Moscow rescue.

Sahidul Barbhuiya, Assam.

Sourabh Pandey, UP.

Sonal Singh at the site of Krishti Chhetri's new home in Jalpaiguri, West Bengal.

Manila rescue.

Ration distribution drive in Sundarban.

Uzbekistan rescue.

ISM College in Kyrgyzstan, from where almost 250 students were flown to India.

12

Serving the Servers

Name: Sahidul Barbhuiya, representing 180 canteen workers
Age: Twenty-plus
Place: Pune/Mumbai
Reason: Stranded without employment
Destination: Guwahati

'Everyone wants to live on top of the mountain, but all the happiness and growth occurs while you're climbing it,' said Andy Rooney, American radio and TV writer.

I'm still climbing.

But at every crevice where my foot rests or on every protruding ledge where I take a break, I meet hordes of new people with multifarious personalities and needs.

On 1 June 2020, a large contingent of 180 boys, who'd lost their jobs in Pune, found its way to Mumbai. Originally hailing from Hailakandi district in Assam, a six-hour drive from Guwahati, they had been working as cooks, helpers and waiters in factory canteens in Pune. But after the lockdown was imposed in March, the canteen shut and they were turfed out of their jobs. For the next three months, with neither employment nor salary, the same boys who'd been whipping up meals and serving hundreds every day, struggled to put together a decent morsel for themselves.

As hopes of the canteen reopening or finding work elsewhere diminished by the day, they knew that it was time to head home, where they'd at least have family and familiar sights awaiting them. Fortunately for them, some of them had heard about the Ghar Bhejo movement and touched base with me through social media on 1 June, after they had reached Mumbai.

As with every new request, this time, too, I was caught off balance, because of the sheer size of this group. Well, we had airlifted 160-plus factory workers from Kochi and successfully escorted them to Odisha. But in the present case, the large number and the long distance from Mumbai to Guwahati posed new difficulties.

Before we could work out the logistics, we were sure of only one thing: the mode of transport would have to be an airlift again. But it wasn't going to be easy. Nor was it going to happen at the snap of a finger. In fact, it finally took almost ten days for the logistics to be worked out satisfactorily.

The first of June was also when Cyclone Nisarga was heading towards Mumbai. So it was stormy all over—in the sea, up in the skies and on land too. It was in this inclement weather that the boys reached Mumbai. Taking shelter below the Tilak Bridge in Kurla, they started sending me a flurry of SOS messages. The harsh, unrelenting downpour added to their woes as they wondered how long they could withstand the fury of nature under a bridge.

We could understand their predicament. The joblessness, near-starvation and insecurities of the last three months, and then to be literally greeted with a storm in Mumbai . . . But I'm guessing they didn't grasp the enormity of the task they'd placed before us. A curly-haired twenty-something boy called Sahidul Barbhuiya, who had appointed himself as the spokesperson of the group, pleaded with me to somehow get them moving homewards. I wanted to, we wanted to. And we weren't resting until we had arranged transport for them. But they were desperate and had also been longing, for days on end, for a decent meal.

We did what had to be done. I first had them taken to a shelter in Chembur, where they were served hot food and water. After that, we asked them all to catch up on their sleep and rest, and to leave things to us to figure out. Some of the boys had spoken about feeling extreme fatigue, which was a cause for concern in COVID times. So apart from providing them with food and shelter, we had to also keep an eye on their health.

Responding to a special request from these boys, I personally went to Chembur to meet and talk to them. They had been so harshly exposed to the dark side of life between March and June that most of them were anxious, worked up and practically on the verge of breaking down. Many confessed that they had called relatives and friends but had been spurned at every turn. It was a dispiriting and demoralizing chapter in their lives.

What added to their plight was the fact that most of them were in their twenties. They were the sole earning members of their families and had been working in Pune from the time they were twelve or thirteen years old. It was a stark close-up of the harsh reality of child labour that exists under our noses even today.

A classic example was that of a twenty-two-year-old who told me that he'd been working since he was thirteen because no one else in his family was equipped to earn a living. His unskilled father did odd jobs, and they were so poor that two square meals a day was a distant dream for them. His mother and younger sister were also unemployed. So it was up to him to cook at the canteen in Pune and send his meagre earnings to his family in Hailakandi. All this from the age of thirteen. They were robbed of their childhood at a very young age.

It was gratifying that my personal visit boosted their morale, that there was something I could do for them for the time they were under our care. It took us ten days, and on 10 June, my team and I succeeded in sending them by air from Mumbai to Guwahati.

After reaching home, Sahidul spoke, once again on behalf of his group, and put his gratitude into words. He said, 'I caught COVID-19 after I reached home and was quarantined. But I have recovered, and I owe my life to Sonu Sir. Had it not been for his timely intervention, I and some of the other members of our group might not have survived. But our troubles haven't ended. Life at home is tough. We have exhausted all our earnings and there's a daily scramble to feed ourselves. However, if life gives me an opportunity, my one intense desire is to return to Mumbai to cook a meal with Sonu Sir. I also want to take out a public rally for him because of the exemplary and sensitive work he has done in rescuing scores of people like me.'

I couldn't fail to notice the sad irony of Sahidul's life. He was a natural cook who could prepare almost any kind of dish. Meat, chicken, vegetarian and even desserts, he could make almost anything. Yet such has been his struggle since the lockdown that he, and many others like him, have had to sometimes survive on bread and water.

Every case disturbs me and each time I hear such stories, I can't believe what I'm learning about the less fortunate. Despite the lockdown, the health concerns and the collapsing global economy, many of us still manage a meal and the comfort of a home. Misery exists outside our doors, and each one of us is duty-bound to alleviate the sufferings of the less privileged.

Let's pay heed to and act on Andy Warhol's words: 'They always say time changes things, but you actually have to change them yourself.'

13

Emergency Landings

Profile: An assortment of students and patients with medical emergencies
Airlifted from: Manila, the Philippines
Destination: New Delhi, Mumbai, Chennai
Number of passengers: 850 + 36

It all begins and ends with the heart. The heart feels, the mind does the work. And the warmth generated as an end-product returns to reside in the heart. I'll borrow from the political activist and philosopher Thomas Paine and say it in seven words: 'Compassion, the fairest associate of the heart.' But along with the heart, my mind has also expanded due to the vast and varied series of experiences I have had over the past few months.

One had heard general comments that India was fast turning into one of the most favoured spots in the world for medical tourism, which is a growing sector. But through write-ups in various newspapers, Wikipedia and other online sources, I got acquainted with some proud statistics.

In mid-2020, India's medical tourism sector was estimated to be worth $5–6 billion. In 2017, just under 5 lakh patients visited India from all over the world, including countries like Australia, Canada, the United Kingdom and the United States, to seek medical care. In November 2019, the *Economic Times* reported that Maharashtra received 27 per cent, Chennai around 15 per cent and Kerala nearly 5–7 per cent of all medical tourists in India.

Medical tourism once meant that patients travelled from less-developed countries to major medical centres in highly developed countries for treatments that were unavailable at home. However, in recent years, the trend has reversed, with those from developed countries travelling to developing countries for affordable and high-quality medical treatments.

I recently discovered that many medical tourists come to India from the Philippines and that many students go from India to the Philippines to study medicine. I had no clue that this South East Asian nation has become a natural choice for Indians seeking medical degrees. I found that more than 8000 Indians study science and medicine there, with the number on the rise.

The Philippines offers reasonably priced education and has a large English-speaking community. It has an expanding presence of Indian businesses and a growing domestic tourist inflow. Add to it the tropical climate, the affordable cost of living—as compared to Australia, Europe and the US—and top it with the air-travel time of 8–12 hours between Manila and the major metros in India.

These factors account for the two-way traffic between India and the Philippines. Indian students go to the Philippines to study, and India has become the prime medical destination for the Filipinos for similar reasons.

During the lockdown, I received a two-pronged request that ultimately led to my bringing four planeloads from the Philippines to India.

On 29 August 2020, I tweeted: '*Jab tak aap sab ghar nahin pahonch jaate, hum koshish karte rahenge.* With you till you are home. Continuing those efforts with the fourth flight for our people from Philippines. Your country is waiting for you. @flyspicejet'.

Our international rescue operations had begun and got fine-tuned with the India-bound flights organized from Kyrgyzstan, Kazakhstan, Uzbekistan and Moscow. As observed earlier, most of the students evacuated from these places were medical students (that there were so many of our kids studying there had been a revelation for me).

With the pandemic enforcing hostels to be shut and universities all over asking students to vacate their premises, we brought many of them home to various cities in India. And that's when we became aware that people in the Philippines were also looking to us for help.

There are statistics available to show that the Philippines had one of the highest cases of infection in South East Asia. A *New York Times* report said that at one point there were nearly 1,70,000 confirmed cases, out of which 30,000 were reported in one week in the month of August.

I got a call that almost 850 medical students needed to be evacuated. We were by now familiar with the procedure to be followed. I spoke to the Indian ambassador and other authorities in the Philippines, impressing upon them how imperative it was to get the students back to India. After several calls, my attempts paid off. I got one planeload out of Manila.

We managed to fly back the entire lot of students by spreading it over a month from August to September, and putting them on six different flights. But even as we were getting the students out, there was another desperate scenario that drew my attention. Once word spread that Sonu and his Ghar Bhejo team had actually got a planeload of students out of Manila, we got an emergency request, asking us to arrange passage for nineteen children who needed to undergo liver transplant surgeries. They were Filipino kids who were scheduled to be operated on in Delhi. However, they had been unsuccessful in getting a flight.

With medical costs being lower in India than in the Philippines, the parents had chosen hospitals in Delhi for their kids. Prior to the lockdown, all of them had secured the necessary permissions after showing their respective medical reports. But once the pandemic and the global lockdown came into effect, their plans went awry. These were medical emergencies; it was a question of their children's lives.

Over the past few months, it wasn't just the COVID-19 virus that killed people; the lockdown imposed because of it also took the lives of many around the world. The children from the Philippines who couldn't get medical help because they couldn't be flown out had no option but to stay back in their own country. It was heart-wrenching to learn that six of them died before they could fly to India. This naturally doubled the stress of the parents/guardians of the thirteen other kids who were on standby. They were anguished and desperate to get their children to operating theatres in India.

When I entered the picture, I managed to organize a flight for all these children. Twenty-six adults were also scheduled to fly with the thirteen minor patients. The adults included parents, attendants and a few donors too.

But once again, my heart took a hit. Even as we were finalizing the last-minute evacuation details, one more child lost the battle and died before he could be put on a plane to India. We could therefore rush to the aid of only a dozen kids. On 15 August, they landed in Delhi along with their guardians and within a couple of days, they were wheeled in for surgery.

I got a lot of thank-you calls from grateful parents. But for us, the uplifting news was that most of the children recouped and responded well to the surgeries. I find it hard to verbalize how difficult it is to deal with emotions when there are so many lives involved, especially those of little children. This 'emergency landing' moved me so much that I didn't know how to grapple with the intensity of my feelings when I learnt about the children who succumbed while waiting for a flight. I could console myself saying that the responsibility was not mine alone, but it hurt because they had once connected with me and I felt that the onus was on me to ensure their safety. I experienced a personal feeling of helplessness when one child died before boarding the flight.

I've heard from some people that real men don't cry. Don't believe it for a minute. The six-pack abs notwithstanding, my heart bleeds and I tear up each time I am faced with a human tragedy. Compassion is an emotion that's compatible with the toughest of exteriors.

14

Laurels for a Portal

On 15 August 2020, I played a new role before the camera. I turned guest anchor on the popular news channel ABP News for a special programme they'd put together for Independence Day.

On 26 August, a social media user called Arunesh Mishra addressed Prime Minister Narendra Modi on Twitter and suggested that an essay on 'Sonu Sood's exemplary social work should be included in the syllabus of school children so that more and more students are inspired to follow suit and emulate him'.

These are just two small examples of the acknowledgement by the media and the public of the humanitarian turn my life has taken, of the social worker avatar of actor Sonu Sood. It is the acclaim given to our continual efforts to rehabilitate a variety of people in dozens of different ways.

While I have been humbled and honoured by all the praise I have received, it has also spurred me to keep going. And everywhere I looked, there was someone calling out to me.

Speaking of someone calling out to me, there was this phase during the lockdown when I was so stretched with requests for help and so deeply involved with getting people's lives back on track that I often had to put my own work on the back burner. Scripts had piled up on my desk. But due to my total involvement in the Ghar Bhejo movement and other work associated with it, I found it virtually impossible to get down to reading the scripts. I was mentally stimulated by the distress calls and, at the same time, I was exhausted. Trying to get myself to concentrate on reading a script became difficult.

Fortunately for me, my producers were more than understanding. They knew that I had a bigger task on hand, one that was tactical and called for immediate action. Once the lockdown ended, I was able to get back to reading my scripts. The simple point here is—we think we are super human, but even the best of us can stretch ourselves thus far and no further. At such times, it's best to concentrate on the job at hand and take a short break from other activities. The idea is to never burn yourself out.

In July, the Twitterati went crazy over the video of an eighty-five-year-old saree-clad lady performing *lathi-kathi*, a warrior dance with bamboo sticks wielded in martial-arts style, on the streets. Wearing a mask—that's what she did to keep body and soul together—she was performing for the few coins that she would collect from onlookers. The clip piqued the interest of many celebrities, who wanted to find out more about this feisty 'Warrior *Aaji*' or 'Warrior Grandma', as she soon came to be known.

I was fascinated by her. My team tracked her down as Shanta Balu Pawar of Pune. Gifting her with cash was a way of encouraging her for the short term. But as always, my endeavour was to gift her a livelihood. When you see such rare talent, you also want it passed on to more people and many more generations. Warrior Aaji was the ideal response to anyone who groaned about their age or used age as a ruse to sit back and do nothing. At eighty-five, Shanta Pawar was animated and alive. We wanted to turn her into an institution of inspiration. As the American actress and activist Jane Fonda said, 'It's never too late, never too late to start over, never too late to be happy.'

On 22 August, the auspicious occasion of Ganesh Chaturthi, we opened Shanta Pawar's martial arts and self defence school in her city, from where she began to dispense her knowledge and train many in her special *lathi baazi*. 'It has been my dream which Sonu has fulfilled,' beamed Aaji that day. Shanta Bai's goal is to impart self-defence techniques to women and children through her martial arts with bamboo sticks.

I was keen to name her new place Shanta Balu Pawar Martial Arts School, but she insisted on naming it after me. So now there's a Sonu Sood Martial Arts School in Pune. Mark that as another place I must visit once our lives return to normal.

August was a month when diverse entreaties were made to me, packing my Twitter timeline. Tucked amid the many petitions for money, tuition fees, medical aid or laptops and books that I received on social media, there would also be the quirky odd request from a Captain Cool fan, asking me to arrange a photograph with Mahendra Singh Dhoni. That moment of amusement aside, there was literally a flood of appeals made to me when floods ravaged the state of Bihar. One request was from a man named Bhola, from Champaran. Misfortune visited him when the raging waters took away his son and his buffalo, his only source of income.

There was no way to compensate him for the loss of his child, but Neeti Goel and I got into the act double quick and bought him a brand-new buffalo. We couldn't restore the life of his child, but we could provide him with a means to earn his livelihood so he could take care of his other children.

It was such a thrill to see the smile back on Bhola's innocent face at the sight of his new buffalo that I couldn't help tweeting, 'I was not as excited buying my first car as I was buying a new buffalo for you. Will drink a glass of fresh buffalo milk when I come to Bihar.'

By a rough estimate, Bhola will now have a minimum income of Rs 20,000 per month, because a buffalo, on an average, gives at least ten litres of milk a day. After deducting the cost of maintaining his animals, Bhola will still have enough cash on hand to take care of his daily needs and that of his family.

'Bounty always receives part of its value from the manner in which it's bestowed,' said the eighteenth-century English writer Samuel Johnson. Whether a buffalo for Bhola in Champaran, a tractor for farmer Nageswara Rao in Chittoor, or a *pucca* bricks-and-cement house for Krishti Chhetri in Jalpaiguri—gifting what someone needs at the right time and with the right grace is the only correct way of giving. Santa's golden rule should always be followed: Bring a smile to another person's face, rather than saying, 'I've done this for you, and now you owe me', a PR stunt that makes the receiver feel like a worm and makes any act of charity lose its pious propriety.

If I strive to make somebody's life better today, sometime in the future, hopefully, they will experience in their turn the bigger joy of giving when they're in a position to help someone else. Let the chain remain unbroken, and may many more ultimately benefit from it. This would be the ultimate gift I could ever hope to receive.

People who receive may be happy, but nothing can match the ecstasy of giving. What you give has a way of coming back to you manifold and in an array of manifestations. I've witnessed a spectacular phenomenon, somewhat akin to the 'butterfly effect', where the flapping of wings in one place can bring about a change somewhere else. Team Ghar Bhejo and I 'flapped our wings' in one small suburb when we flagged off 350 migrants. And look at how it has made a mark all over the world.

Countless NGOs from across India have joined the caravan with great enthusiasm. Like a potluck dinner, some brought their goodwill, others brought capital through crowd-funding sources, and many more just brought whatever they had and put it on the table. I can't count on my fingers the many medical operations where doctors waived away their fees saying, 'Sonu, we're just happy to be of service to you in these hard times.' It was so rewarding to discover so much compassion in so many people.

I want to thank each and every doctor, nurse, social worker, academician, government official, bureaucrat, as well as members of the general public who have joined the movement. This amazing cross section of people have empowered me, shared my responsibilities and lightened the load. Together, what a patchwork quilt we've spread all over.

When it came to requests for help, stark visuals often touched my heart and galvanized me into action. The living conditions of Krishti Chhetri, a twelve-year-old girl from Jalpaiguri in north Bengal, particularly distressed me. Sonal Singh, one of Krishti's neighbours, got on Twitter and showed me the photos of what was 'home' to the child and her unemployed father—a few tattered plastic sheets and gunny bags stitched together. Through winter, rain and summer, this was where father and daughter stayed, facing the toughest of weather and the most pitiable of financial conditions. Krishti's father was among the many who lost employment during the lockdown.

Sonal Singh's tweet made me sit up and go full steam into it. Sitting in Mumbai, I could orchestrate funds and the right people to go and turn that unusable shanty into a proper little house in Jalpaiguri. The concrete house that sprang up within days was a pleasurable sight for Chhetri's neighbours too.

Watching that cement-and-brick dwelling coming up in place of torn plastic sheets and gunny bags, Sonal Singh was moved to say, 'Living 2500 kms away in Mumbai, Sonu Sood has done this for Krishti. I never imagined that a personality as renowned as him would react and respond to my tweet. I'm a simple person, and helping Krishti was beyond my capacity. We'll never forget what he has done for the little girl.'

Another neighbour, Raju Karmakar, remarked, 'We witnessed how the little girl was struggling. She and her father used to stay in the shanty through the monsoon and winter, facing tough situations. This actor, living thousands of kilometres away, responded to her plight. We are grateful to him.'

As an impromptu gesture, they painted these words on a blue tarpaulin and hung it up. It reads:

> *Garibon ka ek hi sahara*
> *Sonu Sood hamara*
> *Beghar ko ghar dene ke liye hum log*
> *Tahe dil se aapko dhanyavaad karte hai*
> *Thank you Sonu Sood*

The brand-new abode, where Krishti and her mother now stay, has a name painted on the outer wall: 'Sonu Sood Niwas'. '*Chalo*, now I can safely say that I have a house even in Jalpaiguri,' I tweeted happily on 21 August. It does look like I will have many places to visit once the pandemic is behind us for good.

But there was no time for complacency as a feeling of helplessness washed over me every time there was a message from a migrant worker I'd sent home. Floods had played havoc in the two states of Assam and Bihar, adding to the hardships of people who were already reeling under unemployment, poverty and insecurity. That awful feeling in the pit of my stomach returned when the labourers I'd sent home to these states got in touch, saying, 'Sir, you got us home, but now we have no means of livelihood. The floods have ruined our lives even further.'

Every time I waved goodbye to a bus or trainload of migrants, at the back of my mind would be the unasked question, 'Will they ever come back to the big cities again?'

A month or two later, I started getting messages from many who wanted to get back to their work in the cities. But all of them aspired to better standards and living conditions. I was looking for employers and industry bodies that would come forward to do something more than provide jobs for the workers.

Neither the pandemic nor nature's fury was under anybody's control. But I stood at the crossroads once again: Should I console myself that I'd done what I could? Or should I wade again towards an unopened door? My mind said, talk, plan, act and think of the future.

I knew that I had to start a dialogue with the state authorities and address issues like the aftermath of the floods. Bring things under control, minimize the damage, rehabilitate.

Simultaneously, Team Ghar Bhejo went into action mode and sent rations to the people of Assam and Bihar. That was the short-term, do-it-now act. However, I knew that this wasn't a permanent solution to the monstrous problem that loomed before us, which wasn't restricted to people missing out on a meal or two.

An open hand as opposed to a tight fist is the posture to adopt for life. But at the same time, while you, I and everybody must help the millions who're miserable, we should also remember these words by John D. Rockefeller Jr: 'Charity is injurious unless it helps the recipient to become independent of it.' That has been the non-stop effort of my 'One-Stop Counter', where empowering every underprivileged person to stand on his or her own feet is the ultimate goal.

Thinking of these varied goals and experiences, I got a good idea of the work that awaited me long after COVID-19 was confined to the pages of history as a nightmare that descended on mankind in 2020. I knew that I had my work cut out for me for the rest of my life. In fact, one lifetime wouldn't be enough.

Once we gauged the mammoth task before us and knew where we had to reach, we began to plot the route. On 23 July, we launched our ambitious project, Pravasi Rojgar, the free mobile app and website in English and Hindi.

Pravasi Rojgar is aimed at going beyond the short term and helping people across the length and breadth of India. Sending rations to the needy was not enough. The 1.5 lakh migrants I'd sent home needed jobs. They needed a permanent source of income to take care of themselves and their loved ones.

This gigantic initiative is all about introducing blue-collar job seekers to the best ways of earning an income and to provide a social-safety net for them, besides facilitating and mentoring their career progression. While looking at a long-term vision, Pravasi Rojgar also tackles the immediate target of providing employment to the millions of migrant workers who have lost their livelihood due to the pandemic.

'Luck is a matter of preparation meeting opportunity,' said the Roman philosopher Seneca. Luck was around the corner for the unemployed migrant as we laid the ground, planning and prepping to bring opportunity to him.

We put in place a five-year plan, which aims at finding employment for and impacting at least 2 crore youths. We looked at a young and varied workforce that could either be migrants who'd left the big cities and gone home, or migrants who wanted to return to the cities, or those who'd passed out of college or school. We also turned our gaze at jobs for dropouts at the entry level in the manufacturing and service sectors. It was the socially and economically backward sections of society, men and women at the bottom of the pyramid, whose lives we wanted to touch, change and improve.

At the end of five years, I wish to see the change we could work in their socio-economic status.

'If you light a lamp for someone else, it will also brighten your path.' The Buddha's wisdom has lit up my life, and that of Team Ghar Bhejo, in unimaginable ways. In the process of interacting with people and exploring new avenues of opportunities for multitudes, our dividends were incalculable too, as we gained through the new vistas of knowledge that had opened out before us. Apart from being warmed by an eternal glow inside our hearts, of course.

Even as we were getting our Pravasi Rojgar app readied, I remembered my own predicament. I had studied to be an engineer. Before I took the plunge into acting, myriad thoughts had danced in my head. When a bolt of pragmatism would strike me, I would ponder, 'Should I seek employment as an engineer or some other safe and secure white-collar job?' Ultimately, when acting happened to me, I realized that jobs were not mechanical choices; they were emotional choices as well. I therefore want those seeking jobs through Pravasi Rojgar to also find emotional sustenance through the professions they find themselves in. Sometime further down the months, when the economy has steadied, it is my ardent wish to emotionally connect with the various job seekers of our country. I hope to see a day when most people are doing the jobs they have a burning passion for, rather than sweating only to keep their kitchen fires burning.

We looked at all sides of the unemployment crisis and calculated that if there were jobless people eager to offer their services, there would be an equal number searching for the right hands to hire. On paper, it was the simple question of bringing together two people who were looking for each other. But implementation required management skills, as we had to source the companies or associations which were facing a severe shortage of skilled workers, step in and enable them to sustain, grow and create more jobs.

We also gave serious thought to the training, assessment and certification of skills of the workers, which would help the companies to increase retention, productivity and consequently, their sustainability. Pravasi Rojgar was started as a holistic portal that would also be of immense help to the government in realizing the social inclusion and economic growth objectives of their initiatives and schemes.

Pravasi Rojgar was thus designed as an online platform where both job seekers and job givers could register themselves. After providing relevant details, those looking for employment can search and apply for openings based on their skill set, industry and location preference. Business owners, on the other hand, can hunt for suitable candidates for their specific work needs. The initiative also caters to the skill-enhancement needs of candidates in order to provide them career advancement opportunities.

The idea behind the website and app was to make the entire process of job searching, filtering and application a hassle-free experience. No more feverish scanning of ads in newspapers or on multiple job sites. As a free mobile app, Pravasi Rojgar is accessible to registered users anytime and anywhere. We wanted to find opportunities for skilled, semi-skilled and unskilled workers. Pravasi Rojgar is for job seekers of all stripes, from DTP operators and drivers to plumbers and accountants.

Pravasi Rojgar went public on 23 July 2020. On 15 August, I ecstatically tweeted, '3,00,000+ jobs committed, 20,000+ interviews in progress.' Through the use of Pravasi Rojgar, 10,000 people have already started their work. This was wrought by a well-thought-out, well-planned and well-executed move to connect with a wide variety of potential employers and others vital to our scheme.

We looked at upscaling the initiative by connecting with 8000–10,000 schools across the country that would help us teach and train thousands of economically disadvantaged people, so that they can be placed in the kinds of jobs they want. I dream of the day Pravasi Rojgar will connect the whole country.

Establishing relationships with employers added credibility to the jobs being offered. For starters, Pravasi Rojgar partnered with some of the top companies across the country from diverse sectors, like construction, health care, logistics, security, agriculture, food processing, call centres, automotive, maintenance and housekeeping, and garment export.

I tied up with the Apparel Export Promotion Council (AEPC), an agency with several garment exporters on its roster, and our understanding with export associations bore fruit almost instantly, in different ways. A round of talks with the AEPC chairman, A. Sakthivel, yielded guaranteed jobs for a good percentage of labour enlisted with Pravasi Rojgar. He promised to provide jobs to around 1,00,000 people, because export orders had started picking up.

We also forged ties with Amazon, the Trident group and dozens of others. The motto was to find jobs for the workers we'd sent home to various states. If they couldn't return to their jobs in big cities like Mumbai, Kolkata, Chennai, Hyderabad and Delhi, we would find them employment closer to their home base. No matter how remote the corner where they lived, we will do our utmost to find them a way to earn a living.

'You don't have to be great to start but you have to start to be great,' said author and motivational speaker Zig Ziglar. When I started Ghar Bhejo, I just took a leap of faith and had my fingers crossed, hoping to succeed in what I had set out to do. However, once the initial part of the mission was executed on a large scale with micro precision, the responsibility didn't recede; it multiplied. After sending people home, other stark truths hit me hard. The challenge was hydra-headed: that omnipresent evil called unemployment, and other basic needs having to do with education for children and medical care for dependants.

Team Ghar Bhejo had to think on its feet as we had to tackle new issues every day. I suddenly had an extended family of more than 1,00,000. When I'd stood at Kalwa Chowk on 15 April with just two associates, I had not envisaged the size and shape this campaign would assume within four months.

'Noida apparel makers tie up with Sonu Sood to woo migrants back,' announced a report filed by Shalabh in the *Times of India*. Pravasi Rojgar, the report said, is a 'symbiotic model that seeks to revive the employer's business and the employee's trust'. 'Bollywood actor Sonu Sood, with the Noida authority with him in an important supporting role, has created what could possibly become a template for large industrial clusters looking to bounce back from the lockdown.'

My conversation with the exporters' association led to the first big success of Pravasi Rojgar as we got a robust job-plus-accommodation offer from the Noida Apparel Export Cluster (NAEC). When the NAEC approached me with an immediate assurance of housing and jobs for 1500 workers, it was the big break I was looking for. If migrants were desperate for work, so were the employers, like the members of the NAEC, who anxiously awaited the return of skilled workers to the shop floors with the festive season closing in. We were promised that it would eventually burgeon into accommodation for 20,000 workers in Noida, allowing migrant workers to return to the city with the assurance of a job and subsidized housing. Since I was looking for businessmen, industrialists, company owners and industry bodies to do something more than provide employment to workers, the proposal appealed to me and I agreed to play catalyst.

Noida is a pilot project, and I aim to replicate this in other cities over the next few months. Gradually, I want to cover the entire stretch across north India and create a similar model. In the next phase, we will launch the scheme in Punjab and Rajasthan. A worker from Jharkhand will ultimately have to move to the NCR or Mumbai in search of greener pastures. Ours is an aspirational India. So, the expectations of workers have also changed, and they want the assurance of better living conditions for themselves, which, in turn, will improve the overall productivity of the industry.

The NAEC came to me because they wanted to use our database of workers. My job was to provide the NAEC with the details of migrant workers and send them to Noida in batches. Our association encountered some roadblocks, the biggest of which was convincing workers to return and assuring them that they wouldn't face another lockdown. Workers, particularly migrants from outside Noida, were also worried about finding a place to live, since pandemic restrictions continued to be in force. Therefore, before approaching me, the NAEC first met Noida Authority officials to thrash out a housing solution for workers.

That will be an ongoing project for the next couple of years. Meanwhile, there were other events that called my attention. Like when I read in the *Indian Express* about the plight of kids in a remote village—Morni, Haryana—who had to travel miles to access a smartphone for online classes, it struck me as grave injustice. Here we were, so used to our phones and high-speed Internet that we tended to take it all for granted. And out there were those kids who had to go miles to attend their online classes. How could I not step in?

As soon as I read the news report, I tweeted, 'No more travelling for these kids. They will have their smartphones by tomorrow.'

On 26 August, the students of the Government Senior Secondary School in Morni received their smartphones through a friend of mine who delivered them to the school principal on my behalf. What an undiluted pleasure it was to talk to the excited kids over a video call.

I had to tweet, 'A wonderful beginning to my day watching all the students get their smartphones to attend their online classes. @karangilhotra, *padega India toh badega India*.

Thanks to @HkinaRohtaki for bringing this need to our notice.'

'In the past few months, the 47-year-old Bollywood actor has not only become an everyday Santa Claus for the disadvantaged and the desperate, he has emerged as India's chief minister of hope,' wrote senior journalist Avijit Ghosh in the *Times of India*. 'Sonu's Twitter timeline is a document of everything India has endured since the nationwide lockdown in March. It's a bulletin board for the jobless, the stranded, and the ailing—ordinary people handcuffed by problems and with nowhere to go. But the model-turned-actor's account— he has 3.2 million followers—is also a heart-tugging story of a film star who walks his tweets. And who doesn't stop walking, even though the lockdown is long gone.'

I bow to that line, 'A film star who walks his tweets', and can't stress enough how much I imbibed from watching my parents' actions. As Mr Ghosh put it, 'The teenager internalised empathy from their actions.' My parents were my school.

There isn't a moment when something doesn't touch your heart, confirming that by stepping forward to help, you're doing something right. As I said earlier, one lifetime isn't enough for what I want to do. But I do know that this lifetime has been earmarked for a dream.

15

A Grandmaster's Move

More than 'House Full' and 'Sold Out', the one signboard that buoys the mood and triggers a happy pirouette displays only three short words, 'We are hiring'. It's music to the ears of the unemployed, especially in an economically depressed post-pandemic world.

Food packets and ticket money were but temporary soothers when lakhs of migrants trekked home to escape the imperative but impoverishing COVID-19 lockdown. Apart from home and health, everyone required one more vital nutrient: a job to wake up to every morning.

It was with a splash of colours that 25 November 2020 turned into a red-letter day for blue-collar workers, with the coming together of GoodWorker, a digital job matching platform, Schoolnet, a leading education and vocational skills provider, and Pravasirojgar.com, which I had launched in July 2020 as an employment portal for job seekers, especially migrants, after millions lost their livelihood due to the nightmarish pandemic.

Within a short spell of four months, my job website and app received an overwhelming response from all stakeholders, onboarding over 10 lakh employment seekers and thousands of employers.

My efforts to empower millions got an invigorating fillip when GoodWork and Schoolnet came on board to form a joint venture with me with an initial investment of Rs 250 crore. It flagged off a season of well-founded, well-grounded optimism, as it signalled self-reliance and growth, the dire needs of the crisis year.

Let me introduce my partners in this life-changing venture. Founded in Singapore by the global investment company Temasek, GoodWork is a job-matching platform that connects blue-collar workers with potential employers. Using decentralized technology built by Affinidi, which was also founded by Temasek, GoodWork has the sharp and sure aim of arming workers and their families with digital identities and verifiable credentials, so that they have greater control of their data while upping their access to employment opportunities and life-empowering services.

My second partner, Schoolnet India Limited (formerly IL&FS Education and Technology Services Ltd), is a market leader in edtech and vocational skilling services, with its presence in 400 districts across India. It has developed innovative technology-enabled solutions for teaching and learning. Through its multi-stakeholder partnerships with governments, private sector, institutions and international agencies, Schoolnet has the capacity to move closer to my goal of maximum reach, scale, impact and sustainability.

Pravasi Rojgar, which I launched, took off, along with Schoolnet, with the clear aim of providing employment opportunities to job seekers in the skill-based work sector, link youths to companies for entry-level jobs and supply mentor support to all of them right through the journey.

Employment is a balm for the job seeker. A glimpse at the profiles of all three partners of this joint venture will give a big-picture view of our combined strengths in migrant outreach, education, skilling and technology—all centred on a core digital platform and a physical network spread across India.

I have to thank Ekam Advisors, an investment banking firm, which was instrumental in bringing all the partners together and advised us on the strategy for such a fulfilling initiative. With this, the caravan grew stronger.

Migrants and displaced workers have taken permanent residence in my heart. Partnering with a socially relevant technology platform will be a restorative for me; it will help me institutionalize and overwhelmingly change the scale of Pravasi Rojgar's humanitarian work. It's like a dream taking flesh-and-blood shape as I spread my job-giving net all over the country to stimulate development through cause-oriented technology.

What I cannot emphasize enough is that this partnership, along with all my other efforts, complements the government's initiatives to spur economic growth and create employment.

COVID-19 treated us all as pawns. But I'll go along with American writer Issac Asimov and say, 'In life, unlike chess, the game continues after checkmate.' The November venture gave me the push to knock the after-effects of the pandemic off the chessboard of life.

16

A Prescription for Enrichment

History is replete with inspiration. Thumb through a book and you come across role models from the past marching by in all colours. But nothing inspires the young as much as a flesh-and-blood exemplar that stands before them and makes them vow, 'I, too, can do what he does.'

Sonia Sotomayor, the first Hispanic member of the Supreme Court of the United States, wrapped it up in language worthy of a lady of justice when she remarked, '. . . But a role model in the flesh provides more than inspiration; his or her very existence is confirmation of possibilities one may have every reason to doubt, saying, "Yes, someone like me can do this."'

It was a similar thought, embedded in an Andhra Pradesh campus, that birthed the idea of naming an entire department after me. When the Sarat Chandra Degree College and Sarat Chandra Junior College rechristened their arts and humanities department as the 'Sonu Sood Department of Arts and Humanities', it wasn't a self-aggrandizing trophy moment for me. Rather, it was about providing the impressionable souls who walked the corridors of that educational institution with a real, reachable and tangible catalyst of social change—a figure who exemplified that they could, and anybody could, be the change that society so vitally required.

As American author and publisher Sheri L. Dew, who was never short of the right words, chose to put it, 'True leaders understand that leadership is not about them but about those they serve. It is not about exalting themselves but about lifting others up.' It true not just of leadership but of any honour bequeathed on you. It speaks of what you stand for—which can be beneficially emulated by all, especially by the malleable young.

Speaking of the young, I must digress and recount the story of Dapana village near Morni, Haryana, where children had to climb trees to study because they had no access to a satellite connection.

A few months ago, Dapana was just another place on the Indian map, one of the less fortunate places with no proper roads, no connectivity and barely any access to the rest of the country. Though it is just fifty-odd kilometres from Chandigarh, this village and its people were cut off because they didn't have good roads enabling travel to the main city. And, no mobile connectivity. Children for whom a network connection is a lifeline, especially with online studies becoming a norm during this pandemic, were in a complete fix.

As Chandigarh-based philanthropist and entrepreneur Karan Gilhotra and I discovered, children there studied at odd hours and that too on tree tops, just to be able to get a signal on their mobiles. Boys and girls alike were climbing trees, sometimes really tall ones, to get those magic-signal bars on their phones.

Their parents couldn't speak to relatives or friends settled elsewhere because of the poor mobile signal. If a relative passed away, they heard about the demise several days later as their phones didn't work.

That's when Karan, Airtel and I combined forces to put up a tower close to this village. Karan told me, 'Sonu, the situation in Morni is disheartening because these simple folk lack basic infrastructure and connectivity. Let us swing into action immediately and put up a mobile tower. I can't imagine, children having to climb trees to study!'

Today, the face of the village has changed. And the worry lines have disappeared from the brows of the beautiful children.

Coming back to having an education department named after me, I could hold forth before a mike or write reams on how humbling and gratifying it was to have such an honour bestowed on me. But truly, I would want the new honour to have a two-fold motivational impact: first, on me, so that I keep extending a hand to those who seek my help; and second, on the students who could mirror my actions, thereby turning themselves into beacons of hope for the marginalized. It was this last hope that drove the institution to put 'Sonu Sood' on the nameplate of the department, as the managing director of the Sarat Chandra IAS Academy testifies. The citation said, 'Sonu Sood has set an example for the young population of the country. We hope to educate our students so that they follow in his footsteps.'

If there was a moment of pride over these golden honours, it lingered only over the thought that a professor who had devoutly dedicated her life to the student world would be smiling with contentment at her son today.

But personally, there wasn't a moment to spare to sit back and reflect on myself with indolence. For I had miles to go and much to do en route.

The pandemic, which had wrought such a change in me, showed no signs of subsiding by November 2020. So the world that had been caught in shock a few months ago, shook itself, came to terms with the implications and went back to restoring its dignity.

For an actor, it meant going back to the studios. After the August–September schedule of *Alludu Adhurs* (the refreshed title of *Kandireega 2*), with director Santosh Srinivas at the helm, the frequency of shoots increased, and my dates diary went back to blocking chunks of my time for my films. But personally, I could never rewind and go back to being who I was before March 2020. Not only had I changed inexorably and irreversibly, so had the circumstances around me.

In November, I was back in Hyderabad, on another schedule of *Alludu Adhurs*, when my colleagues also recorded the unalterable change that my presence had brought to the studio. Replacing the stargazers who stood outside the studio gates for a glimpse of their favourite matinee idols was a desperate wave of humanity. I accepted it as an inevitable constant for the rest of my life and began to admire the discipline with which the crowd organized itself into a queue outside the gates of the Ramoji Rao Film City.

In Mumbai, the road that led to my building had turned into a similar sight as countless families approached my team with unbroken regularity, seeking help for unaffordable medical procedures. Over the last few months, multiple surgeries have been facilitated by our team at the SRCC, Wadia and Kokilaben Dhirubhai Ambani hospitals for a cross section of children and grown-ups. Anguished calls from line producers and crew members within the film industry and from total strangers outside my world had also become a daily feature of our lives.

The same scene was replicated in Hyderabad. We were shooting the climax of *Alludu Adhurs*, with 300 junior artistes at a *mandapam* (a hall booked for weddings and other auspicious ceremonies) in a spacious convention centre. Thanks to the large crew and the huge presence of junior artistes, many more people heard that I was on location. With innumerable interactions on social media, where so many uploaded and disseminated the news of my presence, a herd of humanity flocked to the venue. In between shots, I would walk out to greet the hordes outside with a namaste, which was reassuring for those who ached for an attentive ear.

People would queue up from 5.30 a.m. and wait patiently until 6 p.m. for their turn to meet me with medical reports of their children, partners or other family members. For as many days as the shoot went on, it became a daily ritual for me to report to work, pack up in the evening and spend a minimum of three hours meeting each one in the queue outside. It also meant perusing a ton of medical reports, making on-the-spot assessments and noting down the follow-up action for my Ilaaj India team to take over and actively pursue.

I had to be what people hoped I would be—a medium who'd pull them out of a stressful situation. Every meeting introduced me to new forms of wretchedness visiting people.

One that shocked me with its starkness was the case of thirty-nine-year-old Mallikarjun. At first glimpse, he was a success story, with a well-paying job at an MNC. But when ill health hits you hard, jobs and earnings cease to exist. It was discovered that Mallikarjun had a rare heart condition, which needed emergency medical aid. I learnt, much to my dismay, that he had been trying to reach me on Twitter for quite a few months but, unfortunately, couldn't connect with me. His cry for help must have got lost in the voluminous din of pleas that had jammed my handle.

When he heard that I was in Hyderabad, he came over on a wheelchair, accompanied by his wife. The first thing he said to me was, 'Sonu Sir, I am going to die. The doctors have given me just six months.'

Mallikarjun had a peculiar condition due to which his heartbeat slowed down from time to time. He needed frequent visits to the hospital, to be administered shocks that would increase the pace of his heartbeat. But there was no cure in this line of treatment as his own doctors told him that the shocks could only provide temporary relief.

I was jolted, as if I'd been given a shock, and didn't know how to react to this death sentence. As I have said time and again, you hear so much and you see so much, yet there's always another situation around the corner that stuns you with its enormity. You can never be inured to misery.

However well intentioned, words that are meant to soothe ultimately amount to empty platitudes. Verbally, I could offer them a metaphorical shoulder to cry on. But they needed a more practical balm. In the course of our conversation, Mallikarjun expressed what was playing on his mind. 'Sir,' he said, 'I may not survive. However, I request you to please find my wife a suitable job. Our two children have stopped going to school because of the pandemic and also because we couldn't pay their fees. My family is under financial stress because of the huge payments that had to be made for my treatment. Currently, I'm the sole breadwinner of the family. But after me, my wife will have to provide for them.'

With no time to lose, I moved swiftly into action. To begin with, I sorted out his children's school fees. Then I called for all his medical reports and showed them to specialists at the Apollo and KIMS hospitals in Hyderabad. After poring over them for a fortnight, the doctors at KIMS came up with a solution for Mallikarjun's condition. It was a complicated surgery that took place on 2 November.

'Dr' is not just a prefix; it is sometimes a superpower. The right caregiver may be hard to find, but when you do meet him, he is more than a gift; he is a walking miracle. It was miraculous that Mallikarjun, who expected his life to end, began to recuperate and recover, with the medical team conveying to me their confidence that he would be able to resume normal life in a few months' time. I can't tell you how divine that sounded to me.

The magical wand that was pointed at Mallikarjun was but one example. There was a slew of cases that ranged from the seriously incurable to expensively remediable, but most of them fell under the category of a medical emergency. People from places like Nellore and Vellore gathered at Hyderabad to meet me, armed with their requests for intervention.

Nagaraju, my manager in the south, who has been with me from the beginning of my career, recounted to me his experiences while dealing with the crowds. He encountered tearful eyes on every face that sought a meeting with me, making it impossible for him to turn anyone away. He knew that a personal conversation with me would give them at least the salve of reassurance.

His emotional state was an extension of my own intense feelings, which drove me to meet all of them. Bone-tired after a hard day's work of make-believe, I was numbed by the reality of the humanity that stretched before me. Every evening, I left for my hotel only after 9.30 p.m., because I couldn't disappoint those who were waiting for me.

My dusk-to-nightfall conversations at the studio gates were revelatory. Besides those who came looking for help were some who had come only to greet me face to face, for a personal exchange of namastes. What got them here was not the excitement of sighting a film star but their affection for one who symbolized optimism in times of sorrow. For me, this was a new experience, simultaneously flattering and frightening.

But the one paramount takeaway from my transition of 2020 was that the name Sonu Sood had become a source of inspiration.

To inspire others is my true endeavour in life. At the end, every life is just a story. It's up to each one of us to write an enriching one.

17

Let's Hear It for Team Ghar Bhejo

The biggest drawback about reading a book is that it doesn't come with aural effects. Because every name I take here deserves a drum roll. These are names not of people but of pillars, without whose unflinching support Sonu Sood and his buddy Neeti Goel (also the brainchild of the Ghar Bhejo team formation) could never have performed their super feats or carried the super load on their shoulders. So, let the orchestra amp up its sound in your mind and the paradiddle reach a crescendo as I introduce **My Fabulous Sixteen**.

Take a bow:

K.K. Mookhey

From one man to 600 and more. In 2001, K.K. Mookhey founded Network Intelligence, a cybersecurity firm which kicked off as a one-man operation. Today, he leads a team of

600-plus, with offices spread all over the world. Mookhey has been irreplaceable in running our relief operations in Delhi and Mumbai.

Govind Agarwal

Quietly going far beyond book-keeping, Govind Agarwal, a chartered accountant by profession and a financial transformation consultant with Deloitte India, came forth via Twitter. He tweeted to volunteer his services and brought with him such admirable dedication that within a short spell, he became an indispensable part of our core team. A reliable man on the ground, Govind was always just one call away when the distressed had to be rescued from a tight situation. You know the extent of a man's selflessness when you observe him from the sidelines. Govind was with me on day one; he's still the most involved member. Words fail me but I will say a heartfelt thank you to him for his unfailing dedication.

Ashma

She exemplifies *'sabka saath, sabki khushi'*, equality at all levels, happiness for all. She holds a degree in engineering but is an educator by choice. Ashma is driven by principles that she believes in, holds on to and lives by. She is best defined by her good work, and her motto is, *'Sab ek doosre ki izzat karein'*—respect for all humans and equal opportunities for all, irrespective of gender, religion or caste. Ashma's 'trio of tenets' is acceptance, equality and happiness for every living being.

Pankaj Jalisatgi

Juggling debits and credits is not his only specialty. Pankaj Jalisatgi, my chartered accountant and close associate, also holds a degree in law. CEO of NeoOrbit Consulting Private Limited, a business advisory company, Pankaj's forte is media and entertainment. He was one of the first to step aboard Team Ghar Bhejo and helped me realize my impossible dream of sending migrants home. He meticulously spearheaded on-ground operations by taking charge of organizing all modes of transport—bus, train, air and road—for those we sent home.

Vishal Lamba

'Money can't buy me love,' sang the Beatles. Vishal Lamba, who, like me, is an actor by profession, wants all that money can't buy. And he gets it with the off-camera work he untiringly does through his social service organization, the Lamba Foundation. Once he got to know about my efforts and the Ghar Bhejo movement, he reached out to me and joined us. During the course of our association, Vishal let me glimpse what nestled in his heart when he said to me, 'Sonu, money cannot buy us certain things. And I want only those things.' He referred to the extreme satisfaction one derives from helping the needy, which is far more gratifying than anything materialistic. 'As the purse is emptied, the heart is filled,' said Victor Hugo. Service to others has made our hearts burst with immeasurable joy.

Prashika Dua

Clambering out of the box to think afresh is a specialty that comes naturally to twenty-two-year-old Prashika from Shivpuri, Madhya Pradesh. She may be the youngest warrior in the Sonu Sood army, but challenging internships with well-known service providers have equipped her with exceptional skills. A nimble learner with interpersonal and organizational talents, Prashika's verve for unconventional problem-solving and leadership is gift-wrapped with a smile for everybody around. A trained software engineer and Vahani scholar, she is currently the project manager of my Ilaaj India initiative.

Ajay Dhama

Call it the old boys' network. Ajay Dhama and I have known each other for twenty-five years, ever since our college days in Nagpur. We've been together through thick and thin, and we live in the same building too. He organically became a part of my Ghar Bhejo mission. Ajay was the one who drove me to all those far-flung suburbs for my meetings with migrant workers. Often, when people would gather outside my building, it was Ajay who went down to meet and greet them, and to find out what their needs were. At the height of the pandemic, I received 3000 mails and messages per day on an average, all from people seeking help. It was impossible for me to meet or reply to each of them personally. Ajay was invaluable, as he diligently stepped in and eased my workload.

K.N. Karthikeyan

Karthikeyan is also an IIMA graduate and the co-founder of APOS Algo, a B2B analytics/AI firm. He was part of the Tata Administrative Services, where he held multiple senior management posts. He came to us through his work with Khaana Chahiye, an NGO that distributed over 45 lakh meals during the initial stages of the lockdown.

Suchitra Laxman

Funds and focus are her twin aces. Suchitra Laxman is a strategist and mergers and acquisitions consultant who connected with Ghar Bhejo through her alma mater, the Indian Institute of Management Ahmedabad (IIMA). Suchitra was an important part of the woman force that helped raise Rs 60 lakh for our movement. She's someone who is driven, dedicated and determined to achieve whatever she sharply focuses on.

Ashu Tomar

She invests in and harvests ideas. Another IIM product, Ashu works with a leading investment bank. She activated her alumni network for the migrant cause and undertook operational responsibilities, like arranging transportation and working out technicalities with various state authorities. She was also there to see off the migrants on the ground and continues to work with me on various ideas. A warm friendship has sprung between us along the way.

Chintan Desai

Chintan Desai has also been a friend for over a decade. He's a trusted lieutenant and handles all digital communications with super efficiency. On several occasions, he pitched in to organize rail and road transport. Blessed with a pleasant personality, he was the ideal man to go meet migrants and put them in the right frame of mind. I unabashedly used him as our Goodwill Ambassador.

Gautam and Malvika Sachar

I am writing about them as one unit because they worked as a team. My sister, Malvika, and her husband, Gautam, who are social do-gooders in Moga (my hometown), became a part of Team Ghar Bhejo too. They were front-line workers through the pandemic in Moga and Ludhiana, working selflessly with the municipal and medical authorities in bringing aid to the needy. In fact, because they were literally handling the 'home front', my team and I could spread our efforts out to the rest of the world. I feel blessed to have like-minded persons around me. It makes my journey much more meaningful.

Sumita Salve

She's my wife's sister. But the reason she came on board my Ghar Bhejo team was because she wanted to bring change. The fact of her being a relative never came into play when she became one of the key players of Ilaaj India. Sumita holds an MBA in marketing and finance, and a diploma in computer programming. She brings to the table her vast corporate-sector experience and meticulously arranges the charts drawn up to address the burgeoning medical emergencies. She's an entrepreneur, settled in Nagpur for the last thirty years, and is the main point of contact for Ilaaj India when an SOS situation presents itself.

Janhvi and Sidharth Salve

I am blessed to have a family that has stood by me through the pandemic. My niece Janhvi and nephew Sidharth Salve also became a part of my Ghar Bhejo team, looking into logistics of the students and migrants we ferried back and forth. Again, I am counting them as one unit! Train them young and watch them grow, it's said. I've started, how about you?

The foot soldiers who held the movement together:

Sujata Narasimhan
Ashok Rajpurohit
Sadhu Baijnath
Sofyan Sheikh
Sana Akhtar
Sukhnanda Vohra
Sukanya Roy
Swetha Bindu Therlapu
Celin Ekka
Gauri Sikariya
Chinmay Pardeshi
Shazia Saba
Subhangini
Atharva Gore
Usman J. Khan

Astha Jain
Shalini Mehta
Aarti Nihalani
Sreya Ghose
Jahanvee V. Panchal
Dibyajyoti Mondal
Harsh Sikariya
Pragya Tiwari
Errol Mathias
Paras Soni

We have all been blessed with two hands; use at least one to help others. American writer and orator Robert Ingersoll's famous quote reads, 'The hand that helps is holier than the lips that pray.' I'm fortunate to have been surrounded by an abundance of outstanding friends and well-wishers who thought like Ingersoll and became a part of my squad—showing neither a moment's hesitation nor requiring any persuasion. They sensed that I had taken on an onerous task, one that was as vital as my heartbeat for me. They also realized the magnitude and the massiveness of the operation I was involved in. My heartfelt *dhanyavaad* to every member of Team Ghar Bhejo.

My restaurateur-entrepreneur buddy Neeti Goel and all the others involved in this movement became a formidable force by my side, and Ghar Bhejo rolled forward and moved continents because of team power. Planning, coordinating, executing and contributing selflessly in every way possible, it was the team that truly turned Ghar Bhejo into the Movement of the Year 2020.

18

Forty-Eight Shades of Film

I could also call them my multicultural affairs, for that's how every one of these assignments has been for me—red-hot and passionate. These are the forty-eight movies that came together to make Sonu Sood the celebrity and star; the forty-eight that introduced the 'kulcha from Moga' to a cross section of cultures, cuisines and co-stars, making me the complete Indian, making me Sonu Sood, the actor-producer.

They are also what made me stand out. I know of no other parallel, no other actor who has had as fortuitous a career as I have had. For any actor anywhere in the world, this would be the dream résumé—to have clocked in significant work in five Indian languages (Hindi, Urdu, Tamil, Telugu and Kannada) and in substantial English films outside our national borders too.

Do catch me in the following:

Film: *Kallazhagar* (1999)
Cast: Vijayakanth, Laila, Nassar, **Sonu Sood**

Director: Marumalarchi K. Bharathi
Language: Tamil

Film: *Majunu* (2001)
Cast: Prashanth, Rinky Khanna, **Sonu Sood**, Raghuvaran
Director: Ravichandran
Language: Tamil

Film: *Shaheed-e-Azam* (2002)
Cast: **Sonu Sood**, Manav Vij, Dev Gill
Director: Sukumar Nair
Language: Hindi

Film: *Zindagi Khoobsoorat Hai* (2002)
Cast: Gurdas Mann, Tabu, **Sonu Sood**
Director: Kajal Naskar, Manoj Punj
Language: Hindi

Film: *Ammayilu Abbayilu* (2003)
Cast: Vijaya Sai, Mohit Chadha, **Sonu Sood**
Director: Ravi Babu
Language: Telugu

Film: *Kahan Ho Tum* (2003)
Cast: Ishita Arun, **Sonu Sood**, Sharman Joshi
Director: Vijay Kumar
Language: Hindi

Film: *Yuva* (2004)
Cast: Ajay Devgn, Abhishek Bachchan, **Sonu Sood**, Kareena Kapoor Khan, Rani Mukerji, Esha Deol, Vivek Oberoi

Director: Mani Ratnam
Language: Hindi

Film: *Sheesha* (2005)
Cast: **Sonu Sood**, Neha Dhupia
Director: Ashu Trikha
Language: Hindi

Film: *Chandramukhi* (2005)
Cast: Rajinikanth, Jyothika, Prabhu, Nayanthara, **Sonu Sood**
Director: P. Vasu
Language: Tamil

Film: *Super* (2005)
Cast: Nagarjuna Akkineni, **Sonu Sood**, Ayesha Takia
Director: Puri Jagannadh
Language: Telugu

Film: *Athadu* (2005)
Cast: Mahesh Babu, Trisha Krishnan, Prakash Raj, **Sonu Sood**
Director: Trivikram Srinivas
Language: Telugu

Film: *Aashiq Banaya Aapne* (2005)
Cast: Emraan Hashmi, **Sonu Sood**, Tanushree Dutta
Director: Aditya Datt
Language: Hindi

Film: *Siskiyaan* (2005)
Cast: **Sonu Sood**, Neha Dhupia, Sachin Khedekar

Director: Ashwini Chaudhary
Language: Hindi

Film: *Ashok* (2006)
Cast: N.T. Rama Rao Jr, Sameera Reddy, **Sonu Sood**
Director: Surender Reddy
Language: Telugu

Film: *Rockin' Meera* (2006)
Cast: TQ, **Sonu Sood**, Nauheed Cyrusi
Director: Param Gill
Language: English

Film: *Mr. Medhavi* (2008)
Cast: Raja, Genelia D'Souza, **Sonu Sood**
Director: G. Neelakanta Reddy
Language: Telugu

Film: *Jodhaa Akbar* (2008)
Cast: Hrithik Roshan, Aishwarya Rai Bachchan, **Sonu Sood**
Director: Ashutosh Gowariker
Languages: Hindi, Urdu

Film: *Singh Is Kinng* (2008)
Cast: Akshay Kumar, Katrina Kaif, **Sonu Sood**, Om Puri
Director: Anees Bazmee
Language: Hindi

Film: *Ek Vivaah… Aisa Bhi* (2008)
Cast: **Sonu Sood**, Isha Koppikar

Director: Kaushik Ghatak
Language: Hindi

Film: *Arundhati* (2009)
Cast: Anushka Shetty, **Sonu Sood**, Arjan Bajwa, Sayaji Shinde
Director: Kodi Ramakrishna
Language: Telugu

Film: *Dhoondte Reh Jaoge* (2009)
Cast: Paresh Rawal, Kunal Kemmu, **Sonu Sood**
Director: Umesh Shukla
Language: Hindi

Film: *Anjaneyulu* (2009)
Cast: Ravi Teja, Nayanthara, **Sonu Sood**
Director: Parasuram
Language: Telugu

Film: *Ek Niranjan* (2009)
Cast: Abhinayasri, **Sonu Sood**
Director: Puri Jagannadh
Language: Telugu

Film: *City of Life* (2009)
Cast: Alexandra Maria Lara, **Sonu Sood**, Saoud Al Kaabi
Director: Ali F. Mostafa
Language: English

Film: *Dabangg* (2010)
Cast: Salman Khan, Sonakshi Sinha, Vinod Khanna, **Sonu Sood**

Director: Abhinav Kashyap
Language: Hindi

Film: *Sakthi* (2011)
Cast: N.T. Rama Rao Jr, Ileana D'Cruz, **Sonu Sood**
Director: Meher Ramesh
Language: Telugu

Film: *Teen Maar* (2011)
Cast: Pawan Kalyan, Trisha Krishnan, **Sonu Sood**, Paresh Rawal
Director: Jayanth C. Paranjee
Language: Telugu

Film: *Bbuddah Hoga Terra Baap* (2011)
Cast: Amitabh Bachchan, Hema Malini, **Sonu Sood**
Director: Puri Jagannadh
Language: Hindi

Film: *Kandireega* (2011)
Cast: Ram Pothineni, Hansika Motwani, **Sonu Sood**
Director: Santosh Srinivas
Language: Telugu

Film: *Dookudu* (2011)
Cast: Mahesh Babu, Samantha Ruth Prabhu, **Sonu Sood**
Director: Sreenu Vaitla
Language: Telugu

Film: *Osthe* (2011)
Cast: T.R. Silambarasan, Richa Langella, **Sonu Sood**

Director: Dharani
Language: Tamil

Film: *Vishnuvardhana* (2011)
Cast: Sudeep, Bhavana, Priyamani, **Sonu Sood**
Director: P. Kumar
Language: Kannada

Film: *Maximum* (2012)
Cast: Naseeruddin Shah, **Sonu Sood**, Neha Dhupia
Director: Kabeer Kaushik
Language: Hindi

Film: *Uu Kodathara Ulikki Padathara* (2012)
Cast: Manoj Kumar Manchu, Deeksha Seth, Nandamuri Balakrishna, **Sonu Sood**
Director: Sekhar Raja
Language: Telugu

Film: *Julayi* (2012)
Cast: Allu Arjun, Ileana D'Cruz, **Sonu Sood**
Director: Trivikram Srinivas
Language: Telugu

Film: *Shootout at Wadala* (2013)
Cast: John Abraham, Manoj Bajpayee, **Sonu Sood**
Director: Sanjay Gupta
Language: Hindi

Film: *Ramaiya Vastavaiya* (2013)
Cast: **Sonu Sood**, Girish Kumar, Shruti Haasan, Randhir Kapoor

Director: Prabhudheva
Language: Hindi

Film: *R… Rajkumar* (2013)
Cast: Shahid Kapoor, Sonakshi Sinha, **Sonu Sood**
Director: Prabhudheva
Language: Hindi

Film: *Entertainment* (2014)
Cast: Akshay Kumar, **Sonu Sood**, Tamannaah Bhatia
Director: Sajid–Farhad
Language: Hindi

Film: *Aagadu* (2014)
Cast: Mahesh Babu, Shruti Haasan, **Sonu Sood**
Director: Sreenu Vaitla
Language: Telugu

Film: *Happy New Year* (2014)
Cast: Shah Rukh Khan, Abhishek Bachchan, Deepika Padukone, **Sonu Sood**
Director: Farah Khan Kunder
Language: Hindi

Film: *Xuanzang* (2016)
Cast: Huang Xiaoming, Kent Tong, **Sonu Sood,** Andrew Lin, Ali Fazal, Neha Sharma, Mandana Karimi
Director: Jianqi Huo
Languages: Mandarin, Hindi

Film: *Ishq Positive* (2016)
Cast: Noor Bhukari, Wali Hamid Ali Khan, **Sonu Sood**
Director: Noor Bhukari
Language: Urdu

Film: *Devi* (2016)
Cast: **Sonu Sood**, Tamannaah Bhatia, Prabhudheva
Director: A.L. Vijay
Languages: Hindi, Tamil, Telugu

Film: *Kung Fu Yoga* (2017)
Cast: Jackie Chan, **Sonu Sood**, Disha Patani
Director: Stanley Tong
Languages: Mandarin, English, Hindi

Film: *Paltan* (2018)
Cast: **Sonu Sood**, Jackie Shroff, Arjun Rampal
Director: J.P. Dutta
Language: Hindi

Film: *Simmba* (2018)
Cast: Ranveer Singh, Sara Ali Khan, **Sonu Sood**, Ajay Devgn
(special appearance)
Director: Rohit Shetty
Language: Hindi

Film: *Devi 2* (2019)
Cast: Prabhudheva, Tamannaah Bhatia, **Sonu Sood**
Director: A.L. Vijay
Language: Tamil, Telugu

Author's Acknowledgements

I would like to thank my friends, fans and extended family for all the support, love and guidance given to me during this special journey called life. The pandemic brought me closer to them.

I would like to thank my parents, Saroj and Shakti. My mother had a library, and she inculcated the reading habit in my sisters, Monika and Malvika, and in me. I'm glad that this habit brought me to this juncture. Ideally, I'd like to send a copy of *I Am No Messiah* to my parents in heaven and seek their blessings.

I would like to thank my wife, Sonali, and my two sons, Eshaan and Ayaan. Sonali has stood by me like the Rock of Gibraltar through life's highs, lows and mid-level crises. My boys are my boys—special in every way. They say the child is the father of man. My boys have added that dimension. I learn from them each day.

I would like to thank my sisters, Monika (elder) and Malvika (younger), for making my growing-up years extra special with their love, patience and understanding.

I want to thank Neeti Goel, who walked with me shoulder to shoulder through the pandemic journey. It's because of her that we managed to make some giant strides at a time when almost nothing was moving.

I would like to thank my co-writer, Meena K. Iyer. She has been a friend since long before she became my co-writer. She is brutally honest, calling a spade a spade.

Last but not the least, I would like to thank my publishers, Penguin Random House, and editor, Milee Ashwarya. Milee has been just a phone call away on every occasion that I have needed her.

Mumbai   Sonu Sood
December 2020

Co-author's Acknowledgements

I would like to thank the Google search engine and various news agencies/portals that afforded me a chance to browse endlessly while researching reports and quotations.

I would like to thank my parents, Alamelu and Krishnan, for being my guiding light through life. My sister, Lalitha, for having stood by me during the first forty years of this journey.

I would like to thank my friend Parvez Qureshi for being patient with me during a pandemic. He attended to chores while I worked tirelessly to meet deadlines, even volunteering to read/reread some chapters.

I would also like to thank my guru, Bharathi S. Pradhan. My writing journey began under her in the '80s at the *Eve's Weekly* group.

I would also like to thank Milee Ashwarya at Penguin Random House for her patience and guidance. In age, she's younger, but offers correct insights into the publishing sphere.

Mumbai   Meena K. Iyer
December 2020

List of Sources

Michelle Landy, '"Give it a try" whispered the heart', MichelleLandy.com, accessed on 2 October 2020, http://michellelandy.com/2013/07/give-it-a-try-whispered-the-heart/?doing_wp_cron=1606884077.90556907653 80859375000

Bharathi S Pradhan, 'Some Shine Brighter', Telegraph India. 17 May 2020, accessed on 2 October 2020, https://www.telegraphindia.com/entertainment/coronavirus-how-some-in-the-mumbai-film-industry-have-been-silently-helping-people-during-the-covid-19-lockdown/cid/1773564

'"Ask Not What Your Country Can Do for You . . ."', JFK Library, accessed on 2 October 2020, https://www.jfklibrary.org/learn/education/teachers/curricular-resources/elementary-school-curricular-resources/ask-not-what-your-country-can-do-for-you

Sangeetha Devi Dundoo, 'Sonu Sood: "Migrant Workers Built Our Homes; I Couldn't Watch Them Being Homeless"', *The Hindu*, 29 May 2020, accessed on 2 October 2020, https://www.thehindu.com/entertainment/movies/sonu-sood-migrant-workers-built-our-homes-i-couldnt-watch-them-being-homeless/article31685826.ece

'"I Always Wondered Why Somebody Doesn't Do Something about That. Then I Realised I Was Somebody"—Lily Tomlin', Pinterest, accessed on 2 October 2020, https://in.pinterest.com/pin/358881282643751054/

Lachmi Deb Roy, 'Won't Rest until the Last Migrant Reaches Home: Sonu Sood', *Outlook*, 25 May 2020, accessed on 2 August 2020, https://www.outlookindia.com/website/story/india-news-wont-rest-until-the-last-migrant-reaches-home-sonu-sood/353468

'Faith Is Taking That First Step, Even When You Can't See the Whole Staircase', IFunny, accessed on 2 September 2020, https://ifunny.co/picture/faith-is-taking-that-first-step-even-when-you-can-FempWTBm7

Barkha Dutt, 'The Power of One. Actor @SonuSood (Also Aided by His Friend Neeti), Send Hundreds of Migrant Workers Home, First to Karnataka & Now to U.P. One Bus Costs Anywhere between 65,000 and 2 Lakh Rupees. Catch His Story on @themojo_in Https://t.co/N0rsBbqhng', Twitter, 17 May 2020, accessed on 2 September 2020, https://twitter.com/BDUTT/status/1261916287522881536

Divyesh Singh, '"Mahatma" Sonu Sood Will Soon Meet PM Modi: Shiv Sena Attacks Actor over His Help to

Migrants', *India Today*, 7 June 2020, accessed on 2 September 2020, https://www.indiatoday.in/india/story/ sonu-sood-mahatma-narendra-modi-mann-ki-baat-shiv-sena-saamana-migrants-1686434-2020-06-07

'"Good Work Sonu", Says Punjab CM on Actor's Charity', Sahara Samay, accessed on 2 September 2020, http://m. saharasamay.com/entertainment-news/676622706/-good-work-sonu-says-punjab-cm-on-actor-s-charity. html

'Sonu Sood Most Popular in IIHB Survey on Celebrity Performance during Lockdown', Exchange4Media, accessed on 2 September 2020, https://www. exchange4media.com/marketing-news/sonu-sood-most-popular-in-survey-on-celebrity-performance-during-lockdown-105802.html

Malcolm Gladwell, *Outliers: The Story of Success* (London: Penguin Books, 2009)

'Irving Berlin – The Song Is Ended (But the Melody Lingers On)', Genius.com, accessed on 2 September 2020, https://www.genius.com/Irving-berlin-the-song-is-ended-but-the-melody-lingers-on-lyrics

'Quotes On "Grief" That Made Me Accept Grief', Aesha's Musings, 11 March 2019, accessed on 2 October 2020, https://aeshasmusings.com/musings/quotes-on-grief-that-made-me-accept-grief/

John Green, *The Fault in Our Stars* (New York: Dutton Books, 2018)

John Gray, *Men Are from Mars, Women Are from Venus* (London: Collins Educational, 2005)

'Every Day Thousands of People Ask for Help from Sonu Sood, the Actor Released Figures for the First Time', Dailyhunt.in, accessed on 2 October 2020, https://m. dailyhunt.in/news/africa/english/newscrab-epaper-newcrb/every day thousands of people ask for help from sonu sood the actor released figures for the first time-newsid-n208100608

'Sonu Sood Says JEE-NEET Issue an Exam for Govt, Asks for 60-day Postponement', *India Today*, 26 August 2020, accessed on 2 October 2020, https://www. indiatoday.in/education-today/news/story/sonu-sood-says-jee-neet-issue-an-exam-for-govt-asks-for-60-day-postponement-1715319-2020-08-26

Sonu Sood, 'This Is Not an Examination Only for Students. It's an Examination for the Government Too. Govt. Has an Opportunity to Excel by Postponing #JEE_NEET for 60 Days. Make It Happen and Bring Those Smiles Back. Students & Govt. Can Prepare in This Time Window. #PostponeJEE_NEET', Twitter, 26 August 2020, accessed on 2 October 2020, https://twitter.com/ SonuSood/status/1298543702357336064

'"Can't Waste a Year": Supreme Court Rejects NEET, JEE Delay', Latest Laws, accessed on 2 October 2020, https:// www.latestlaws.com/latest-news/can-t-waste-a-year-supreme-court-rejects-neet-jee-delay/

'NEET, JEE on Time, Number of Exam Centres Increased. 99 per Cent Candidates to Get Their First Choice of Centre Cities', TheRealKashmir.com, 25 August 2020, accessed on 2 October 2020, https://therealkashmir.com/

neet-jee-on-time-number-of-exam-centres-increased-99-per-cent-candidates-to-get-their-first-choice-of-centre-cities/#:~:text=NTA said it has ensured,of NEET (UG) 2020

'IIT-Delhi Issues Guidelines for JEE (Advanced) 2020', *Telangana Today*, 25 September 2020, accessed on 2 October 2020, https://telanganatoday.com/iit-delhi-issues-guidelines-for-jee-advanced-2020

'Sonu Sood Helps Students of Haryana, Sends Them Smartphones to Attend Online Classes', Times Now News, accessed on 2 September 2020, https://www.timesnownews.com/education/article/sonu-sood-sends-smartphones-to-students-of-haryana-to-attend-online-classes/643053

'Mitch Albom: Quotes', Goodreads, accessed on 2 October 2020, https://www.goodreads.com/quotes/426515-behind-all-your-stories-is-always-your-mother-s-story-because

'A Quote by Oliver Wendell Holmes Sr.', Goodreads, accessed on 2 November 2020, https://www.goodreads.com/quotes/60651-youth-fades-love-droops-the-leaves-of-friendship-fall-a

'Rabindranath Tagore: Best 20 Quotes For You', TheSocians.com, 14 February 2020, accessed on 2 August 2020, https://www.thesocians.com/post/rabindranath-tagore-best-20-quotes-for-you#:~:text=Go not to the temple to pray on bended knees,who have sinned against you

Debbie Augenthaler, 'Fathers, Angels, and Our Wonderful World: Grief to Gratitude: You Are Not Alone –

A Heartfelt Guide for Grief, Healing, and Hope', DebbieAugenthaler.com, 20 September 2019, accessed on 2 October 2020, https://www.debbieaugenthaler.com/fathers-angels-wonderful-world/

'Sonu Sood to Launch an Initiative for IAS Aspirants, Netizens Hail the Actor', Republic World, 12 October 2020, accessed on 2 November 2020, https://www.republicworld.com/entertainment-news/bollywood-news/sonu-sood-all-set-to-launch-an-initiative-for-ias-aspirants.html

'Sonu Sood Launches "ILAAJ India" Initiative', Goa Chronicle, accessed on 2 October 2020, https://goachronicle.com/sonu-sood-launches-ilaaj-india-initiative/

'Opinion: Sonu Soods UNDP Award Makes His Personal Brand Even Taller', ETBrandEquity.com, 29 September 2020, accessed on 2 October 2020, https://brandequity.economictimes.indiatimes.com/news/marketing/opinion-sonu-soods-undp-award-makes-his-personal-brand-even-taller/78376281

'Medical Tourism Companies Turn to Telemedicine in Wake of Covid-19', Hindustan Times, 16 May 2020, accessed on 2 September 2020, https://www.hindustantimes.com/cities/medical-tourism-companies-turn-to-telemedicine-in-wake-of-covid-19/story-YA0OpXnbjgmvZfsRoHObRP.html

'Stunning Martial Art Moves Of 85-year-old Warrior Aaji Maa From Pune', YouTube, 25 July 2020, accessed on 2 October 2020, https://www.youtube.com/watch?v=8uakXlEOkoI

'12-year-old Girl in Bengal Gets New Home Courtesy Actor
    Sonu Sood', *New Indian Express*, 24 August 2020, accessed
    on 2 October 2020, https://www.newindianexpress.com/
    good-news/2020/aug/24/12-year-old-girl-in-bengal-
    gets-new-home-courtesy-actor-sonu-sood-2187413.html

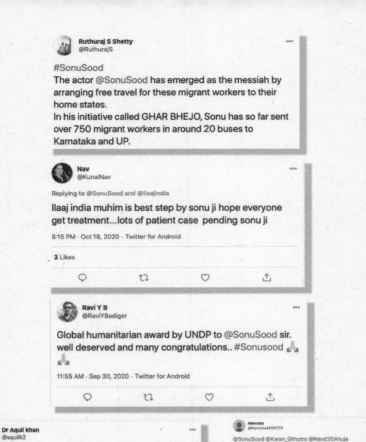

Ruthuraj S Shetty
@RuthurajS

#SonuSood
The actor @SonuSood has emerged as the messiah by arranging free travel for these migrant workers to their home states.
In his initiative called GHAR BHEJO, Sonu has so far sent over 750 migrant workers in around 20 buses to Karnataka and UP.

Nav
@KunalNav

Replying to @SonuSood and @IlaajIndia

Ilaaj india muhim is best step by sonu ji hope everyone get treatment...lots of patient case pending sonu ji

5:15 PM · Oct 18, 2020 · Twitter for Android

3 Likes

Ravi Y B
@RaviYBadiger

Global humanitarian award by UNDP to @SonuSood sir. well deserved and many congratulations.. #Sonusood 🙏
🙏

11:55 AM · Sep 30, 2020 · Twitter for Android

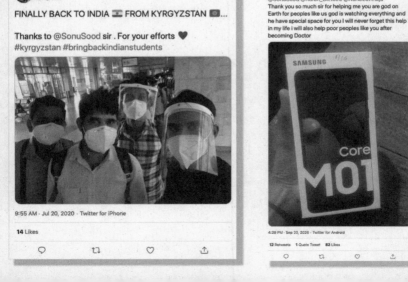

Dr Aquil khan
@aquilk2

FINALLY BACK TO INDIA 🇮🇳 FROM KYRGYZSTAN 🇰🇬...

Thanks to @SonuSood sir . For your efforts 🖤
#kyrgyzstan #bringbackindianstudents

9:55 AM · Jul 20, 2020 · Twitter for iPhone

14 Likes

Namrata
@Namrata44191773

@SonuSood @Karan_Gilhotra @Nand20Ahuja
Thank you so much sir for helping me you are god on Earth for peoples like us god is watching everything and he have special space for you I will never forget this help in my life i will also help poor peoples like you after becoming Doctor

4:28 PM · Sep 20, 2020 · Twitter for Android

12 Retweets   1 Quote Tweet   82 Likes